D1513473

1 3 5 7 9 10 8 6 4 2

Vintage
20 Vauxhall Bridge Road,
London SW1V 2SA

Vintage Classics is part of the Penguin Random House
group of companies whose addresses can be found at
global.penguinrandomhouse.com.

Penguin
Random House
UK

The stories in this edition previously appeared in the *New Yorker*

First published in Great Britain by Jonathan Cape, by arrangement with Alfred
A. Knopf, Inc in 1979
First published by Vintage in 1990
This short edition published by Vintage in 2017

penguin.co.uk/vintage

A CIP catalogue record for this book is available from the British Library

ISBN 9781784872649

Typeset in 9.5/14.5 pt FreightText Pro
by Jouve (UK), Milton Keynes
Printed and bound by Clays Ltd, St Ives plc

Penguin Random House is committed to a sustainable future for
our business, our readers and our planet. This book is made from
Forest Stewardship Council® certified paper.

Drinking

JOHN CHEEVER

VINTAGE MINIS

The Sorrows of Gin

IT WAS SUNDAY afternoon, and from her bedroom Amy could hear the Beardens coming in, followed a little while later by the Farquarsons and the Parminters. She went on reading *Black Beauty* until she felt in her bones that they might be eating something good. Then she closed her book and went down the stairs. The living room door was shut, but through it she could hear the noise of loud talk and laughter. They must have been gossiping or worse, because they all stopped talking when she entered the room.

'Hi, Amy,' Mr Farquarson said.

'Mr Farquarson spoke to you, Amy,' her father said.

'Hello, Mr Farquarson,' she said. By standing outside the group for a minute, until they had resumed their conversation, and then by slipping past Mrs Farquarson, she was able to swoop down on the nut dish and take a handful.

'Amy!' Mr Lawton said.

'I'm sorry, Daddy,' she said, retreating out of the circle, toward the piano.

'Put those nuts back,' he said.

'I've handled them, Daddy,' she said.

'Well, pass the nuts, dear,' her mother said sweetly. 'Perhaps someone else would like nuts.'

Amy filled her mouth with the nuts she had taken, returned to the coffee table, and passed the nut dish.

'Thank you, Amy,' they said, taking a peanut or two.

'How do you like your new school, Amy?' Mrs Bearden asked.

'I like it,' Amy said. 'I like private schools better than public schools. It isn't so much like a factory.'

'What grade are you in?' Mr Bearden asked.

'Fourth,' she said.

Her father took Mr Parminter's glass and his own, and got up to go into the dining room and refill them. She fell into the chair he had left vacant.

'Don't sit in your father's chair, Amy,' her mother said, not realizing that Amy's legs were worn out from riding a bicycle, while her father had done nothing but sit down all day.

As she walked toward the French doors, she heard her mother beginning to talk about the new cook. It was a good example of the interesting things they found to talk about.

'You'd better put your bicycle in the garage,' her father said, returning with the fresh drinks. 'It looks like rain.'

Amy went out onto the terrace and looked at the sky, but it was not very cloudy, it wouldn't rain, and his advice, like all the advice he gave her, was superfluous. They were always at her. 'Put your bicycle away.' 'Open the door for Grandmother, Amy.' 'Feed the cat.' 'Do your homework.' 'Pass the nuts.' 'Help Mrs Bearden with her parcels.' 'Amy, please try and take more pains with your appearance.'

They all stood, and her father came to the door and called her. 'We're going over to the Parminters' for supper,' he said. 'Cook's here, so you won't be alone. Be sure and go to bed at eight like a good girl. And come and kiss me good night.'

After their cars had driven off, Amy wandered through the kitchen to the cook's bedroom beyond it and knocked on the door. 'Come in,' a voice said, and when Amy entered, she found the cook, whose name was Rosemary, in her bathrobe, reading the Bible. Rosemary smiled at Amy. Her smile was sweet and her old eyes were blue. 'Your parents have gone out again?' she asked. Amy said that they had, and the old woman invited her to sit down. 'They do seem to enjoy themselves, don't they? During the four days I've been here, they've been out every night, or had people in.' She put the Bible face down on her lap and smiled, but not at Amy. 'Of course, the drinking that goes on here is all sociable, and what your parents do is none of my business, is it? I worry about drink more than most people, because of my poor sister. My poor sister drank too much. For ten years, I went to visit her on Sunday afternoons, and most of the time she was *non compos mentis*. Sometimes I'd find her huddled up on the floor with one or two sherry bottles empty beside her. Sometimes she'd seem sober enough to a stranger, but I could tell in a second by the way she spoke her words that she'd drunk enough not to be herself any more. Now my poor sister is gone, I don't have anyone to visit at all.'

'What happened to your sister?' Amy asked.

'She was a lovely person, with a peaches-and-cream complexion and fair hair,' Rosemary said. 'Gin makes some people gay – it makes them laugh and cry – but with my sister it only made her sullen and withdrawn. When she was drinking, she would retreat into herself. Drink made her contrary. If I'd say the weather was fine, she'd tell me I was wrong. If I'd say it was raining, she'd say it was clearing. She'd correct me about everything I said, however small it was. She died in Bellevue Hospital one summer while I was working in Maine. She was the only family I had.'

The directness with which Rosemary spoke had the effect on Amy of making her feel grown, and for once politeness came to her easily. 'You must miss your sister a great deal,' she said.

'I was just sitting here now thinking about her. She was in service, like me, and it's lonely work. You're always surrounded by a family, and yet you're never a part of it. Your pride is often hurt. The Madams seem condescending and inconsiderate. I'm not blaming the ladies I've worked for. It's just the nature of the relationship. They order chicken salad, and you get up before dawn to get ahead of yourself, and just as you've finished the chicken salad, they change their minds and want crab-meat soup.'

'My mother changes her mind all the time,' Amy said.

'Sometimes you're in a country place with nobody else in help. You're tired, but not too tired to feel lonely. You go out onto the servants' porch when the pots and pans are done, planning to enjoy God's creation, and although the front of the house may have a fine view of the lake or the mountains, the view from the back is never much. But there is the sky and the trees and the stars and the birds singing and the pleasure of resting your feet. But then you hear them in the front of the house, laughing and talking with their guests and their sons and daughters. If you're new and they whisper, you can be sure they're talking about you. That takes all the pleasure out of the evening.'

'Oh,' Amy said.

'I've worked all kinds of places – places where there were eight or nine in help and places where I was expected to burn the rubbish myself, on winter nights, and shovel the snow. In a house where there's a lot of help, there's usually some devil among them – some old butler or parlormaid – who tries to make your life miserable from the beginning. 'The Madam doesn't like it this way,' and 'The Madam doesn't like it that way,' and 'I've been with the Madam for twenty years,' they tell you. It takes a diplomat to get along. Then there is the rooms they give you, and every one of them I've ever seen is cheerless. If you have a bottle in your suitcase, it's a terrible temptation in the beginning not to

take a drink to raise your spirits. But I have a strong character. It was different with my poor sister. She used to
complain about nervousness, but, sitting here thinking
about her tonight, I wonder if she suffered from nervousness at all. I wonder if she didn't make it all up. I wonder if
she just wasn't meant to be in service. Toward the end, the
only work she could get was out in the country, where
nobody else would go, and she never lasted much more
than a week or two. She'd take a little gin for her nervousness, then a little for her tiredness, and when she'd drunk
her own bottle and everything she could steal, they'd hear
about it in the front part of the house. There was usually a
scene, and my poor sister always liked to have the last
word. Oh, if I had had my way, they'd be a law against it! It's
not my business to advise you to take anything from
your father, but I'd be proud of you if you'd empty his gin
bottle into the sink now and then – the filthy stuff! But it's
made me feel better to talk with you, sweetheart. It's made
me not miss my poor sister so much. Now I'll read a little
more in my Bible, and then I'll get you some supper.'

THE LAWTONS HAD had a bad year with cooks – there had
been five of them. The arrival of Rosemary had made
Marcia Lawton think back to a vague theory of dispensa-
tions; she had suffered, and now she was being rewarded.
Rosemary was clean, industrious, and cheerful, and her
table – as the Lawtons said – was just like the Chambord.
On Wednesday night after dinner, she took the train to

New York, promising to return on the evening train Thursday. Thursday morning, Marcia went into the cook's room. It was a distasteful but a habitual precaution. The absence of anything personal in the room – a package of cigarettes, a fountain pen, an alarm clock, a radio, or anything else that could tie the old woman to the place – gave her the uneasy feeling that she was being deceived, as she had so often been deceived by cooks in the past. She opened the closet door and saw a single uniform hanging there and, on the closet floor, Rosemary's old suitcase and the white shoes she wore in the kitchen. The suitcase was locked, but when Marcia lifted it, it seemed to be nearly empty.

Mr Lawton and Amy drove to the station after dinner on Thursday to meet the eight-sixteen train. The top of the car was down, and the brisk air, the starlight, and the company of her father made the little girl feel kindly toward the world. The railroad station in Shady Hill resembled the railroad stations in old movies she had seen on television, where detectives and spies, bluebeards and their trusting victims, were met to be driven off to remote country estates. Amy liked the station, particularly toward dark. She imagined that the people who traveled on the locals were engaged on errands that were more urgent and sinister than commuting. Except when there was a heavy fog or a snowstorm, the club car that her father traveled on seemed to have the gloss and the monotony of the rest of his life. The locals that ran at odd hours belonged to a world of deeper contrasts, where she would like to live.

They were a few minutes early, and Amy got out of the car and stood on the platform. She wondered what the fringe of string that hung above the tracks at either end of the station was for, but she knew enough not to ask her father, because he wouldn't be able to tell her. She could hear the train before it came into view, and the noise excited her and made her happy. When the train drew in to the station and stopped, she looked in the lighted windows for Rosemary and didn't see her. Mr Lawton got out of the car and joined Amy on the platform. They could see the conductor bending over someone in a seat, and finally the cook arose. She clung to the conductor as he led her out to the platform of the car, and she was crying. 'Like peaches and cream,' Amy heard her sob. ''A lovely, lovely person.' The conductor spoke to her kindly, put his arm around her shoulders, and eased her down the steps. Then the train pulled out, and she stood there drying her tears. 'Don't say a word, Mr Lawton,' she said, 'and I won't say anything.' She held out a small paper bag. 'Here's a present for you, little girl.'

'Thank you, Rosemary,' Amy said. She looked into the paper bag and saw that it contained several packets of Japanese water flowers.

Rosemary walked toward the car with the caution of someone who can hardly find her way in the dim light. A sour smell came from her. Her best coat was spotted with mud and ripped in the back. Mr Lawton told Amy to get in the back seat of the car, and made the cook sit in front, beside him. He slammed the car door shut after her angrily, and then went around to the driver's seat and drove home. Rosemary reached into her handbag and took out a Coca-Cola bottle with a cork stopper and took a drink. Amy could tell by the smell that the Coca-Cola bottle was filled with gin.

'Rosemary!' Mr Lawton said.

'I'm lonely,' the cook said. 'I'm lonely, and I'm afraid, and it's all I've got.'

He said nothing more until he had turned into their drive and brought the car around to the back door. 'Go and get your suitcase, Rosemary,' he said. 'I'll wait here in the car.'

As soon as the cook had staggered into the house, he told Amy to go in by the front door. 'Go upstairs to your room and get ready for bed.'

Her mother called down the stairs when Amy came in, to ask if Rosemary had returned. Amy didn't answer. She went to the bar, took an open gin bottle, and emptied it into the pantry sink. She was nearly crying when she encountered her mother in the living room, and told her that her father was taking the cook back to the station.

When Amy came home from school the next day, she found a heavy, black-haired woman cleaning the living room. The car Mr Lawton usually drove to the station was at the garage for a checkup, and Amy drove to the station with her mother to meet him. As he came across the station platform, she could tell by the lack of color in his face that he had had a hard day. He kissed her mother, touched Amy on the head, and got behind the wheel.

'You know,' her mother said, 'there's something terribly wrong with the guest-room shower.'

'Damn it, Marcia,' he said, 'I wish you wouldn't always greet me with bad news!'

His grating voice oppressed Amy, and she began to fiddle with the button that raised and lowered the window.

'Stop that, Amy!' he said.

'Oh, well, the shower isn't important,' her mother said. She laughed weakly.

'When I got back from San Francisco last week,' he said, 'you couldn't wait to tell me that we need a new oil burner.'

'Well, I've got a part-time cook. That's good news.'

'Is she a lush?' her father asked.

'Don't be disagreeable, dear. She'll get us some dinner and wash the dishes and take the bus home. We're going to the Farquarsons'.'

'I'm really too tired to go anywhere,' he said.

'Who's going to take care of me?' Amy asked.

'You always have a good time at the Farquarsons',' her mother said.

'Well, let's leave early,' he said.

'Who's going to take care of me?' Amy asked.

'Mrs Henlein,' her mother said.

When they got home, Amy went over to the piano.

Her father washed his hands in the bathroom off the hall and then went to the bar. He came into the living room holding the empty gin bottle. 'What's her name?' he asked.

'Ruby,' her mother said.

'She's exceptional. She's drunk a quart of gin on her first day.'

'Oh dear!' her mother said. 'Well, let's not make any trouble now.'

'Everybody is drinking my liquor,' her father shouted, 'and I am God-damned sick and tired of it!'

'There's plenty of gin in the closet,' her mother said. 'Open another bottle.'

'We paid that gardener three dollars an hour and all he did was sneak in here and drink up my Scotch. The sitter we had before we got Mrs Henlein used to water my bourbon, and I don't have to remind you about Rosemary. The cook before Rosemary not only drank everything in my liquor cabinet but she drank all the rum, kirsch, sherry, and wine that we had in the kitchen for cooking. Then, there's that Polish woman we had last summer. Even that old laundress. *And* the painters. I think they must have put some kind of a mark on my door. I think the agency must have checked me off as an easy touch.'

'Well, let's get through dinner, and then you can speak to her.'

'The hell with that!' he said. 'I'm not going to encourage people to rob me. *Ruby!*' He shouted her name several times, but she didn't answer. Then she appeared in the dining-room doorway anyway, wearing her hat and coat.

'I'm sick,' she said. Amy could see that she was frightened.

'I should think that you would be,' her father said.

'I'm sick,' the cook mumbled, 'and I can't find anything around here, and I'm going home.'

'Good,' he said. 'Good! I'm through with paying people to come in here and drink my liquor.'

The cook started out the front way, and Marcia Lawton followed her into the front hall to pay her something. Amy had watched this scene from the piano bench, a position that was withdrawn but that still gave her a good view. She saw her father get a fresh bottle of gin and make a shaker of Martinis. He looked very unhappy.

'Well,' her mother said when she came back into the room. 'You know, she didn't look drunk.'

'Please don't argue with me, Marcia,' her father said. He poured two cocktails, said 'Cheers,' and drank a little. 'We can get some dinner at Orpheo's,' he said.

'I suppose so,' her mother said. 'I'll rustle up something for Amy.' She went into the kitchen, and Amy opened her music to 'Reflets d'Automne.' 'COUNT,' her music teacher had written. 'COUNT and lightly, lightly . . .' Amy began to play. Whenever she made a mistake, she said 'Darn it!' and started at the beginning again. In the middle of 'Reflets d'Automne' it struck her that *she* was the one who had emptied the gin bottle. Her perplexity was so intense that she stopped playing, but her feelings did not go beyond perplexity, although she did not have the strength to continue playing the piano. Her mother relieved her. 'Your supper's in the kitchen, dear,' she said. 'And you can take a popsicle out of the deep freeze for dessert. Just one.'

Marcia Lawton held her empty glass toward her husband, who filled it from the shaker. Then she went upstairs. Mr Lawton remained in the room, and, studying her father closely, Amy saw that his tense look had begun to soften. He did not seem so unhappy any more, and as she passed him on her way to the kitchen, he smiled at her tenderly and patted her on the top of the head.

When Amy had finished her supper, eaten her popsicle, and exploded the bag it came in, she returned to the piano and played 'Chopsticks' for a while. Her father came downstairs in his evening clothes, put his drink on the mantelpiece, and went to the French doors to look at his terrace and his garden. Amy noticed that the transformation that had begun with a softening of his features was even more advanced. At last, he seemed happy. Amy wondered if he was drunk, although his walk was not unsteady. If anything, it was more steady.

Her parents never achieved the kind of rolling, swinging gait that she saw impersonated by a tightrope walker in the circus each year while the band struck up 'Show Me the Way to Go Home' and that she liked to imitate herself sometimes. She liked to turn round and round and round on the lawn, until, staggering and a little sick, she would whoop, 'I'm drunk! I'm a drunken man!' and reel over the grass, righting herself as she was about to fall and finding

At last, he seemed happy. Amy wondered if he was drunk

herself not unhappy at having lost for a second her ability
to see the world. But she had never seen her parents like
that. She had never seen them hanging on to a lamppost
and singing and reeling, but she had seen them fall down.
They were never indecorous – they seemed to get more
decorous and formal the more they drank – but sometimes
her father would get up to fill everybody's glass and he
would walk straight enough but his shoes would seem to
stick to the carpet. And sometimes, when he got to the
dining-room door, he would miss it by a foot or more.
Once, she had seen him walk into the wall with such
force that he collapsed onto the floor and broke most of
the glasses he was carrying. One or two people laughed,
but the laughter was not general or hearty, and most of
them pretended that he had not fallen down at all. When
her father got to his feet, he went right on to the bar as if
nothing had happened. Amy had once seen Mrs Farquarson miss the chair she was about to sit in, by a foot, and
thump down onto the floor, but nobody laughed then, and
they pretended that Mrs Farquarson hadn't fallen down at
all. They seemed like actors in a play. In the school play,
when you knocked over a paper tree you were supposed to
pick it up without showing what you were doing, so that
you would not spoil the illusion of being in a deep forest,
and that was the way *they* were when somebody fell down.

Now her father had that stiff, funny walk that was so
different from the way he tramped up and down the station platform in the morning, and she could see that he

was looking for something. He was looking for his drink. It was right on the mantelpiece, but he didn't look there. He looked on all the tables in the living room. Then he went out onto the terrace and looked there, and then he came back into the living room and looked on all the tables again. Then he went back onto the terrace, and then back over the living room tables, looking three times in the same place, although he was always telling her to look intelligently when she lost her sneakers or her raincoat. 'Look for it, Amy,' he was always saying. 'Try and remember where you left it. I can't buy you a new raincoat every time it rains.' Finally he gave up and poured himself a cocktail in another glass. 'I'm going to get Mrs Henlein,' he told Amy, as if this were an important piece of information.

Amy's only feeling for Mrs Henlein was indifference, and when her father returned with the sitter, Amy thought of the nights, stretching into weeks – the years, almost – when she had been cooped up with Mrs Henlein. Mrs Henlein was very polite and was always telling Amy what was ladylike and what was not. Mrs Henlein also wanted to know where Amy's parents were going and what kind of a party it was, although it was none of her business. She always sat down on the sofa as if she owned the place, and talked about people she had never even been introduced to, and asked Amy to bring her the newspaper, although she had no authority at all.

When Marcia Lawton came down, Mrs Henlein wished

her good evening. 'Have a lovely party,' she called after the Lawtons as they went out the door. Then she turned to Amy. 'Where are your parents going, sweetheart?

'But you must know, sweetheart. Put on your thinking cap and try and remember. Are they going to the club?'

'No,' Amy said.

'I wonder if they could be going to the Trenchers',' Mrs Henlein said. 'The Trenchers' house was lighted up when we came by.'

'They're not going to the Trenchers',' Amy said. 'They hate the Trenchers.'

'Well, where are they going, sweetheart?' Mrs Henlein asked.

'They're going to the Farquarsons',' Amy said.

'Well, that's all I wanted to know, sweetheart,' Mrs Henlein said. 'Now get me the newspaper and hand it to me politely. *Politely*,' she said, as Amy approached her with the paper. 'It doesn't mean anything when you do things for your elders unless you do them politely.' She put on her glasses and began to read the paper.

Amy went upstairs to her room. In a glass on her table were the Japanese flowers that Rosemary had brought her, blooming stalely in water that was colored pink from the dyes. Amy went down the back stairs and through the kitchen into the dining room. Her father's cocktail things were spread over the bar. She emptied the gin bottle into the pantry sink and then put it back where she had found it. It was too late to ride her bicycle and too early to go to bed, and she knew that if she got anything interesting on the television, like a murder, Mrs Henlein would make her turn it off. Then she remembered that her father had brought her home from his trip West a book about horses, and she ran cheerfully up the back stairs to read her new book.

It was after two when the Lawtons returned. Mrs Henlein, asleep on the living-room sofa dreaming about a dusty attic, was awakened by their voices in the hall. Marcia Lawton paid her, and thanked her, and asked if anyone had called, and then went upstairs. Mr Lawton was in the dining room, rattling the bottles around. Mrs Henlein, anxious to get into her own bed and back to sleep, prayed that he wasn't going to pour himself another drink, as they so often did. She was driven home night after night by drunken gentlemen. He stood in the door of the dining room, holding an empty bottle in his hand. 'You must be stinking, Mrs Henlein,' he said.

'Hmm,' she said. She didn't understand.

'You drank a full quart of gin,' he said.

The lackluster old woman – half between wakefulness and sleep – gathered together her bones and groped for her gray hair. It was in her nature to collect stray cats, pile the bathroom up to the ceiling with interesting and valuable newspapers, rouge, talk to herself, sleep in her underwear in case of fire, quarrel over the price of soup bones, and have it circulated around the neighborhood that when she finally died in her dusty junk heap, the mattress would be full of bankbooks and the pillow stuffed with hundred-dollar bills. She had resisted all these rich temptations in order to appear a lady, and she was repaid by being called a common thief. She began to scream at him.

'You take that back, Mr Lawton! You take back every one of those words you just said! I never stole anything in my whole life, and nobody in my family ever stole anything, and I don't have to stand here and be insulted by a drunk man. Why, as for drinking, I haven't drunk enough to fill an eyeglass for twenty-five years. Mr Henlein took me to a place of refreshment twenty-five years ago, and I drank two Manhattan cocktails that made me so sick and dizzy that I've never liked the stuff ever since. How dare you speak to me like this! Calling me a thief and a drunken woman! Oh, you disgust me – you disgust me in your ignorance of all the trouble I've had. Do you know what I had for Christmas dinner last year? I had a bacon sandwich. Son of a bitch!' She began to weep. 'I'm glad I said it!' she screamed. 'It's the first time I've used a dirty word in my whole life and I'm glad I said it. Son of a bitch!' A sense of liberation, as if she stood at the bow of a great ship, came over her. 'I lived in this neighborhood my whole life. I can remember when it was full of good farming people and there was fish in the rivers. My father had four acres of sweet meadowland and a name that was known far and wide, and on my mother's side I'm descended from patroons, Dutch nobility. My mother was the spit and image of Queen Wilhelmina. You think you can get away

with insulting me, but you're very, very, very much mis-
taken.' She went to the telephone and, picking up the
receiver, screamed, 'Police! Police! Police! This is Mrs
Henlein, and I'm over at the Lawtons'. He's drunk, and
he's calling me insulting names, and I want you to come
over here and arrest him!'

The voices woke Amy, and, lying in her bed, she per-
ceived vaguely the pitiful corruption of the adult world;
how crude and frail it was, like a piece of worn burlap,
patched with stupidities and mistakes, useless and ugly,
and yet they never saw its worthlessness, and when you
pointed it out to them, they were indignant. But as the
voices went on and she heard the cry 'Police! Police!' she
was frightened. She did not see how they could arrest her,
although they could find her fingerprints on the empty
bottle, but it was not her own danger that frightened her
but the collapse, in the middle of the night, of her father's
house. It was all her fault, and when she heard her father
speaking into the extension telephone in the library, she
felt sunk in guilt. Her father tried to be good and kind –
and, remembering the expensive illustrated book about
horses that he had brought her from the West, she had to
set her teeth to keep from crying. She covered her head
with a pillow and realized miserably that she would have to
go away. She had plenty of friends from the time when they
used to live in New York, or she could spend the night in
the Park or hide in a museum. She would have to go away.

'GOOD MORNING,' HER father said at breakfast. 'Ready for a good day!' Cheered by the swelling light in the sky, by the recollection of the manner in which he had handled Mrs Henlein and kept the police from coming, refreshed by his sleep, and pleased at the thought of playing golf, Mr Lawton spoke with feeling, but the words seemed to Amy offensive and fatuous; they took away her appetite, and she slumped over her cereal bowl, stirring it with a spoon. 'Don't slump, Amy,' he said. Then she remembered the night, the screaming, the resolve to go. His cheerfulness refreshed her memory. Her decision was settled. She had a ballet lesson at ten, and she was going to have lunch with Lillian Towele. Then she would leave.

Children prepare for a sea voyage with a toothbrush and a Teddy bear; they equip themselves for a trip around the world with a pair of odd socks, a conch shell, and a thermometer; books and stones and peacock feathers, candy bars, tennis balls, soiled handkerchiefs, and skeins of old string appear to them to be the necessities of travel, and Amy packed, that afternoon, with the impulsiveness of her kind. She was late coming home from lunch, and her gateway was delayed, but she didn't mind. She could catch one of the late-afternoon locals; one of the cooks' trains. Her father was playing golf and her mother was off somewhere. A part-time worker was cleaning the living room. When Amy had finished packing, she went into her parents' bedroom and flushed the toilet. While the water murmured, she took a twenty-dollar bill from her mother's desk. Then she went downstairs and left the house and walked around Blenhollow Circle and down Alewives Lane to the station. No regrets or goodbyes formed in her mind. She went over the names of the friends she had in the city, in case she decided not to spend the night in a museum. When she opened the door of the waiting room, Mr Flanagan, the stationmaster, was poking his coal fire.

'I want to buy a ticket to New York,' Amy said.

'One-way or round-trip?'

'One-way, please.'

Mr Flanagan went through the door into the ticket office and raised the glass window. 'I'm afraid I haven't got a half-fare ticket for you, Amy,' he said. 'I'll have to write one.'

'That's all right,' she said. She put the twenty-dollar bill on the counter.

'And in order to change that,' he said, 'I'll have to go over to the other side. Here's the four-thirty-two coming in now, but you'll be able to get the five-ten.' She didn't protest, and went and sat beside her cardboard suitcase, which was printed with European hotel and place names. When the local had come and gone, Mr Flanagan shut his glass window and walked over the footbridge to the north-bound platform and called the Lawtons'. Mr Lawton had just come in from his game and was mixing himself a cocktail. 'I think your daughter's planning to take some kind of a trip,' Mr Flanagan said.

It was dark by the time Mr Lawton got down to the

station. He saw his daughter through the station window. The girl sitting on the bench, the rich names on her paper suitcase, touched him as it was in her power to touch him only when she seemed helpless or when she was very sick. Someone had walked over his grave! He shivered with longing, he felt his skin coarsen as when, driving home late and alone, a shower of leaves on the wind crossed the beam of his headlights, liberating him for a second at the most from the literal symbols of his life – the buttonless shirts, the vouchers and bank statements, the order blanks, and the empty glasses. He seemed to listen – God knows for what. Commands, drums, the crackle of signal fires, the music of the glockenspiel – how sweet it sounds on the Alpine air – singing from a tavern in the pass, the honking of wild swans; he seemed to smell the salt air in the churches of Venice. Then, as it was with the leaves, the power of her figure to trouble him was ended; his goose-flesh vanished. He was himself. Oh, why should she want to run away? Travel – and who knew better than a man who spent three days of every fortnight on the road – was a world of overheated plane cabins and repetitious magazines, where even the coffee, even the champagne, tasted of plastics. How could he teach her that home sweet home was the best place of all?

Goodbye, My Brother

WE ARE A family that has always been very close in spirit. Our father was drowned in a sailing accident when we were young, and our mother has always stressed the fact that our familial relationships have a kind of permanence that we will never meet with again. I don't think about the family much, but when I remember its members and the coast where they lived and the sea salt that I think is in our blood, I am happy to recall that I am a Pommeroy – that I have the nose, the coloring, and the promise of longevity – and that while we are not a distinguished family, we enjoy the illusion, when we are together, that the Pommeroys are unique. I don't say any of this because I'm interested in family history or because this sense of uniqueness is deep or important to me but in order to advance the point that we are loyal to one another in spite of our differences, and that any rupture in this loyalty is a source of confusion and pain.

We are four children; there is my sister Diana and the

three men – Chaddy, Lawrence, and myself. Like most families in which the children are out of their twenties, we have been separated by business, marriage, and war. Helen and I live on Long Island now, with our four children. I teach in a secondary school, and I am past the age where I expect to be made headmaster – or principal, as we say – but I respect the work. Chaddy, who has done better than the rest of us, lives in Manhattan, with Odette and their children. Mother lives in Philadelphia, and Diana, since her divorce, has been living in France, but she comes back to the States in the summer to spend a month at Laud's Head. Laud's Head is a summer place on the shore of one of the Massachusetts islands. We used to have a cottage there, and in the twenties our father built the big house. It stands on a cliff above the sea and, excepting St Tropez and some of the Apennine villages, it is my favorite place in the world. We each have an equity in the place and we contribute some money to help keep it going.

Our youngest brother, Lawrence, who is a lawyer, got a job with a Cleveland firm after the war, and none of us saw him for four years. When he decided to leave Cleveland and go to work for a firm in Albany, he wrote Mother that he would, between jobs, spend ten days at Laud's Head, with his wife and their two children. This was when I had planned to take my vacation – I had been teaching summer school – and Helen and Chaddy and Odette and Diana were all going to be there, so the family would be together. Lawrence is the member of the family with whom the rest of us have least in common. We have never seen a great deal of him, and I suppose that's why we still call him Tifty – a nickname he was given when he was a child, because when he came down the hall toward the dining room for breakfast, his slippers made a noise that sounded like 'Tifty, tifty, tifty.' That's what Father called him, and so did everyone else. When he grew older, Diana sometimes used to call him Little Jesus, and Mother often called him the Croaker. We had disliked Lawrence, but we looked forward to his return with a mixture of apprehension and loyalty, and with some of the joy and delight of reclaiming a brother.

LAWRENCE CROSSED OVER from the mainland on the four-o'clock boat one afternoon late in the summer, and Chaddy and I went down to meet him. The arrivals and departures of the summer ferry have all the outward signs that suggest a voyage – whistles, bells, hand trucks, reunions, and the smell of brine – but it is a voyage of no import, and when I watched the boat come into the blue harbor that afternoon and thought that it was completing a voyage of no import, I realized that I had hit on exactly the kind of observation that Lawrence would have made. We looked for his face behind the windshields as the cars drove off the boat, and we had no trouble in recognizing him. And we ran over and shook his hand and clumsily kissed his wife and the children. 'Tifty!' Chaddy shouted. 'Tifty!' It is difficult to judge changes in the appearance of a brother, but both Chaddy and I agreed, as we drove back to Laud's Head, that Lawrence still looked very young. He got to the house first, and we took the suitcases out of his car. When I came in, he was standing in the living room, talking with Mother and Diana. They were in their best clothes and all their jewelry, and they were welcoming him extravagantly, but even then, when everyone was endeavoring to seem most affectionate and at a time when these endeavors come easiest, I was aware of a faint tension in the room. Thinking about this as I carried Lawrence's heavy suitcases up the stairs, I realized that our dislikes are as deeply ingrained as our better passions, and I remembered that once, twenty-five years ago, when I had hit Lawrence on the head with a rock, he had picked himself up and gone directly to our father to complain.

I carried the suitcases up to the third floor, where Ruth, Lawrence's wife, had begun to settle her family. She is a thin girl, and she seemed very tired from the journey, but when I asked her if she didn't want me to bring a drink upstairs to her, she said she didn't think she did.

When I got downstairs, Lawrence wasn't around, but the others were all ready for cocktails, and we decided to go ahead. Lawrence is the only member of the family who has never enjoyed drinking. We took our cocktails onto the terrace, so that we could see the bluffs and the sea and the islands in the east, and the return of Lawrence and his wife, their presence in the house, seemed to refresh our responses to the familiar view; it was as if the pleasure they would take in the sweep and the color of that coast, after such a long absence, had been imparted to us. While we were there, Lawrence came up the path from the beach.

'Isn't the beach fabulous, Tifty?' Mother asked. 'Isn't it fabulous to be back? Will you have a Martini?'

'I don't care,' Lawrence said. 'Whiskey, gin – I don't care what I drink. Give me a little rum.'

'We don't have any *rum*,' Mother said. It was the first note of asperity. She had taught us never to be indecisive, never to reply as Lawrence had. Beyond this, she is deeply concerned with the propriety of her house, and anything irregular by her standards, like drinking straight rum or bringing a beer can to the dinner table, excites in her a conflict that she cannot, even with her capacious sense of humor, surmount. She sensed the asperity and worked to repair it. 'Would you like some Irish, Tifty dear?' she said. 'Isn't Irish what you've always liked? There's some Irish on the sideboard. Why don't you get yourself some Irish?' Lawrence said that he didn't care. He poured himself a Martini, and then Ruth came down and we went in to dinner.

In spite of the fact that we had, through waiting for Lawrence, drunk too much before dinner, we were all anxious to put our best foot forward and to enjoy a peaceful time. Mother is a small woman whose face is still a striking reminder of how pretty she must have been, and whose conversation is unusually light, but she talked that evening about a soil-reclamation project that is going on up-island.

Diana is as pretty as Mother must have been; she is an animated and lovely woman who likes to talk about the dissolute friends that she has made in France, but she talked that night about the school in Switzerland where she had left her two children. I could see that the dinner had been planned to please Lawrence. It was not too rich, and there was nothing to make him worry about extravagance.

After supper, when we went back onto the terrace, the clouds held that kind of light that looks like blood, and I was glad that Lawrence had such a lurid sunset for his homecoming. When we had been out there a few minutes, a man named Edward Chester came to get Diana. She had met him in France, or on the boat home, and he was staying for ten days at the inn in the village. He was introduced to Lawrence and Ruth, and then he and Diana left.

'Is that the one she's sleeping with now?' Lawrence asked.

'What a horrid thing to say!' Helen said.

'You ought to apologize for that, Tifty,' Chaddy said.

'I don't know,' Mother said tiredly. 'I don't know, Tifty. Diana is in a position to do whatever she wants, and I don't ask sordid questions. She's my only daughter. I don't see her often.'

'Is she going back to France?'

'She's going back the week after next.'

Lawrence and Ruth were sitting at the edge of the terrace, not in the chairs, not in the circle of chairs. With his mouth set, my brother looked to me then like a Puritan cleric. Sometimes, when I try to understand his frame of mind, I think of the beginnings of our family in this country, and his disapproval of Diana and her lover reminded me of this. The branch of the Pommeroys to which we belong was founded by a minister who was eulogized by Cotton Mather for his untiring abjuration of the Devil. The Pommeroys were ministers until the middle of the nineteenth century, and the harshness of their thought – man is full of misery, and all earthly beauty is lustful and corrupt – has been preserved in books and sermons. The temper of our family changed somewhat and became more lighthearted, but when I was of school age, I can remember a cousinage of old men and women who seemed to hark back to the dark days of the ministry and to be animated by perpetual guilt and the deification of the scourge. If you are raised in this atmosphere – and in a sense we were – I think it is a trial of the spirit to reject its habits of guilt, self-denial, taciturnity, and penitence, and it seemed to me to have been a trial of the spirit in which Lawrence had succumbed.

'Is that Cassiopeia?' Odette asked.

'No, dear,' Chaddy said. 'That isn't Cassiopeia.'

'Who was Cassiopeia?' Odette said.

'She was the wife of Cepheus and the mother of Andromeda,' I said.

'The cook is a Giants fan,' Chaddy said. 'She'll give you even money that they win the pennant.'

It had grown so dark that we could see the passage of light through the sky from the lighthouse at Cape Heron. In the dark below the cliff, the continual detonations of the surf sounded. And then, as she often does when it is getting dark and she has drunk too much before dinner, Mother began to talk about the improvements and additions that would someday be made on the house, the wings and bathrooms and gardens.

'This house will be in the sea in five years,' Lawrence said.

'Tifty the Croaker,' Chaddy said.

'Don't call me Tifty,' Lawrence said.

'Little Jesus,' Chaddy said.

'The sea wall is badly cracked,' Lawrence said. 'I looked at it this afternoon. You had it repaired four years ago, and it cost eight thousand dollars. You can't do that every four years.'

'Please, Tifty,' Mother said.

'Facts are facts,' Lawrence said, 'and it's a damned-fool idea to build a house at the edge of the cliff on a sinking coastline. In my lifetime, half the garden has washed away and there's four feet of water where we used to have a bathhouse.'

'Let's have a very *general* conversation,' Mother said bitterly. 'Let's talk about politics or the boat-club dance.'

'As a matter of fact,' Lawrence said, 'the house is probably in some danger now. If you had an unusually high sea, a hurricane sea, the wall would crumble and the house would go. We could all be drowned.'

'I can't *bear* it,' Mother said. She went into the pantry and came back with a full glass of gin.

I have grown too old now to think that I can judge the sentiments of others, but I was conscious of the tension between Lawrence and Mother, and I knew some of the history of it. Lawrence couldn't have been more than sixteen years old when he decided that Mother was frivolous, mischievous, destructive, and overly strong. When he had determined this, he decided to separate himself from her. He was at boarding school then, and I remember that he did not come home for Christmas. He spent Christmas with a friend. He came home very seldom after he had made his unfavorable judgment on Mother, and when he did come home, he always tried, in his conversation, to remind her of his estrangement. When he married Ruth, he did not tell Mother. He did not tell her when his children were born. But in spite of these principled and lengthy exertions he seemed, unlike the rest of us, never to have enjoyed any separation, and when they are together, you feel at once a tension, an unclearness.

And it was unfortunate, in a way, that Mother should have picked that night to get drunk. It's her privilege, and she doesn't get drunk often, and fortunately she wasn't bellicose, but we were all conscious of what was happening. As she quietly drank her gin, she seemed sadly to be parting from us; she seemed to be in the throes of travel. Then her mood changed from travel to injury, and the few remarks she made were petulant and irrelevant. When her glass was nearly empty, she stared angrily at the dark air in front of her nose, moving her head a little, like a fighter. I knew that there was not room in her mind then for all the injuries that were crowding into it. Her children were stupid, her husband was drowned, her servants were thieves, and the chair she sat in was uncomfortable. Suddenly she put down her empty glass and interrupted Chaddy, who was talking about baseball. 'I know one *thing*,' she said hoarsely. 'I know that if there is an afterlife, I'm going to have a very different kind of family. I'm going to have nothing but fabulously rich, witty, and enchanting children.' She got up and, starting for the door, nearly fell. Chaddy caught her and helped her up the stairs. I could hear their tender good nights, and then Chaddy came back. I thought that Lawrence by now would be tired from his journey and his return, but he remained on the terrace, as if he were waiting to see the final malfeasance, and the rest of us left him there and went swimming in the dark.

WHEN I WOKE the next morning, or half woke, I could hear the sound of someone rolling the tennis court. It is a fainter and a deeper sound than the iron buoy bells off the point – an unrhythmic iron chiming – that belongs in my mind to the beginnings of a summer day, a good portent. When I went downstairs, Lawrence's two kids were in the living room, dressed in ornate cowboy suits. They are frightened and skinny children. They told me their father was rolling the tennis court but that they did not want to go out because they had seen a snake under the doorstep. I explained to them that their cousins – all the other children – ate breakfast in the kitchen and that they'd better run along in there. At this announcement, the boy began to cry. Then his sister joined him. They cried as if to go in the kitchen and eat would destroy their most precious rights. I told them to sit down with me. Lawrence came in, and I asked him if he wanted to play some tennis. He said no, thanks, although he thought he might play some singles with Chaddy. He was in the right here, because both he and Chaddy play better tennis than I, and he did play some singles with Chaddy after breakfast, but later on, when the others came down to play family doubles, Lawrence disappeared. This made me cross – unreasonably so, I suppose – but we play darned interesting family doubles and he could have played in a set for the sake of courtesy.

Late in the morning, when I came up from the court alone, I saw Tifty on the terrace, prying up a shingle from the wall with his jack-knife. 'What's the matter, Lawrence?' I said. 'Termites?' There are termites in the wood and they've given us a lot of trouble.

He pointed out to me, at the base of each row of shingles, a faint blue line of carpenter's chalk. 'This house is about twenty-two years old,' he said. 'These shingles are about two hundred years old. Dad must have bought shingles from all the farms around here when he built the place, to make it look venerable. You can still see the carpenter's chalk put down where these antiques were nailed into place.'

It was true about the shingles, although I had forgotten it. When the house was built, our father, or his architect, had ordered it covered with lichened and weather-beaten shingles. I didn't follow Lawrence's reasons for thinking that this was scandalous.

'And look at these doors,' Lawrence said. 'Look at these doors and window frames.' I followed him over to a big Dutch door that opens onto the terrace and looked at it. It was a relatively new door, but someone had worked hard to conceal its newness. The surface had been deeply scored with some metal implement, and white paint had been rubbed into the incisions to imitate brine, lichen, and weather rot. 'Imagine spending thousands of dollars to make a sound house look like a wreck,' Lawrence said. 'Imagine the frame of mind this implies. Imagine wanting to live so much in the past that you'll pay men carpenters' wages to disfigure your front door.' Then I remembered Lawrence's sensitivity to time and his sentiments and opinions about our feelings for the past. I had heard him say, years ago, that we and our friends and our part of the nation, finding ourselves unable to cope with the problems of the present, had, like a wretched adult, turned back to what we supposed was a happier and a simpler time, and that our taste for reconstruction and candlelight was a measure of this irremediable failure. The faint blue line of chalk had reminded him of these ideas, the scarified door had reinforced them, and now clue after clue presented itself to him – the stern light at the door, the bulk of the chimney, the width of the floorboards and the pieces set into them to resemble pegs. While Lawrence was lecturing me on these frailties, the others came up from the court. As soon as Mother saw Lawrence, she responded, and I saw that there was little hope of any rapport between the matriarch and the changeling. She took Chaddy's arm. 'Let's go swimming and have Martinis on the beach,' she said. 'Let's have a *fabulous* morning.'

The sea that morning was a solid color, like verd stone. Everyone went to the beach but Tifty and Ruth. 'I don't mind *him*,' Mother said. She was excited, and she tipped her glass and spilled some gin into the sand. 'I don't mind *him*. It doesn't matter to me how *rude* and *horrid* and *gloomy* he is, but what I can't bear are the faces of his wretched little children, those fabulously unhappy little children.' With the height of the cliff between us, everyone talked wrathfully about Lawrence; about how he had grown worse instead of better, how unlike the rest of us he was, how he endeavored to spoil every pleasure. We drank our gin; the abuse seemed to reach a crescendo, and then, one by one, we went swimming in the solid green water. But when we came out no one mentioned Lawrence unkindly; the line of abusive conversation had been cut, as if swimming had the cleansing force claimed for baptism. We dried our hands and lighted cigarettes, and if Lawrence was mentioned, it was only to suggest, kindly, something that might please him. Wouldn't he like to sail to Barin's cove, or go fishing?

And now I remember that while Lawrence was visiting us, we went swimming oftener than we usually do, and I think there was a reason for this. When the irritability that accumulated as a result of his company began to lessen our patience, not only with Lawrence but with one another, we would all go swimming and shed our animus in the cold water. I can see the family now, smarting from Lawrence's rebukes as they sat on the sand, and I can see them wading and diving and surface-diving and hear in their voices the restoration of patience and the rediscovery of inexhaustible good will. If Lawrence noticed this change – this illusion of purification – I suppose that he would have found in the vocabulary of psychiatry, or the mythology of the Atlantic, some circumspect name for it, but I don't think he noticed the change. He neglected to name the curative powers of the open sea, but it was one of the few chances for diminution that he missed.

The cook we had that year was a Polish woman named Anna Ostrovick, a summer cook. She was first-rate – a big, fat, hearty, industrious woman who took her work seriously. She liked to cook and to have the food she cooked appreciated and eaten, and whenever we saw her, she always urged us to eat. She cooked hot bread – crescents and brioches – for breakfast two or three times a week, and she would bring these into the dining room herself and say, 'Eat, eat, eat!' When the maid took the serving dishes back into the pantry, we could sometimes hear Anna, who was standing there, say, 'Good! They eat.' She fed the garbage man, the milkman, and the gardener. 'Eat!' she told them. 'Eat, eat!' On Thursday afternoons, she went to the movies with the maid, but she didn't enjoy the movies, because the actors were all so thin. She would sit in the dark theater for an hour and a half watching the screen anxiously for the appearance of someone who had enjoyed his food. Bette Davis merely left with Anna the impression of a woman who has not eaten well. 'They are all so skinny,' she would say when she left the movies. In the evenings, after she had gorged all of us, and washed the pots and pans, she would collect the table scraps and go out to feed the creation. We had a few chickens that year, and although they would have roosted by then, she would dump food into their troughs and urge the sleeping fowl to eat. She fed the songbirds in the orchard and the chipmunks in the yard. Her appearance at the edge of the garden and her urgent voice – we could hear her calling 'Eat, eat, eat' – had become, like the sunset gun at the boat club and the passage of light from Cape Heron, attached to that hour. 'Eat, eat, eat,' we could hear Anna say. 'Eat, eat . . .' Then it would be dark.

When Lawrence had been there three days, Anna called me into the kitchen. 'You tell your mother,' she said, 'that *he* doesn't come into my kitchen. If *he* comes into my kitchen all the time, I go. *He* is always coming into my kitchen to tell me what a sad woman I am. He is always telling me that I work too hard and that I don't get paid enough and that I should belong to a union with vacations. Ha! He is so skinny but he is always coming into my kitchen when I am busy to pity me, but I am as good as him, I am as good as *anybody*, and I do not have to have people like that getting into my way all the time and feeling sorry for me. I am a famous and a wonderful cook and I have jobs everywhere and the only reason I come here to work this summer is because I was never before on an island, but I can have other jobs tomorrow, and if he is always coming into my kitchen to pity me, you tell your mother I am going. I am as good as *anybody* and I do not have to have that skinny all the time telling how poor I am.'

I was pleased to find that the cook was on our side, but I felt that the situation was delicate. If Mother asked Lawrence to stay out of the kitchen, he would make a grievance out of the request. He could make a grievance out of anything, and it sometimes seemed that as he sat darkly at the dinner table, every word of disparagement, wherever it was aimed, came home to him. I didn't mention the cook's complaint to anyone, but somehow there wasn't any more trouble from that quarter.

The next cause for contention that I had from Lawrence came over our backgammon games.

When we are at Laud's Head, we play a lot of backgammon. At eight o'clock, after we have drunk our coffee, we usually get out the board. In a way, it is one of our pleasantest hours. The lamps in the room are still unlighted, Anna can be seen in the dark garden, and in the sky above her head there are continents of shadow and fire. Mother turns on the light and rattles the dice as a signal. We usually play three games apiece, each with the others. We play for money, and you can win or lose a hundred dollars on a game, but the stakes are usually much lower. I think that Lawrence used to play – I can't remember – but he doesn't play any more. He doesn't gamble. This is not because he is poor or because he has any principles about gambling but because he thinks the game is foolish and a waste of time. He was ready enough, however, to waste his time watching the rest of us play. Night after night, when the game began, he pulled a chair up beside the board, and watched the checkers and the dice. His expression was scornful, and yet he watched carefully. I wondered why he watched us night after night, and, through watching his face, I think that I may have found out.

Lawrence doesn't gamble, so he can't understand the excitement of winning and losing money. He has forgotten how to play the game, I think, so that its complex odds can't interest him. His observations were bound to include the facts that backgammon is an idle game and a game of chance, and that the board, marked with points, was a symbol of our worthlessness. And since he doesn't understand gambling or the odds of the game, I thought that what interested him must be the members of his family. One night when I was playing with Odette – I had won thirty-seven dollars from Mother and Chaddy – I think I saw what was going on in his mind.

Odette has black hair and black eyes. She is careful never to expose her white skin to the sun for long, so the striking contrast of blackness and pallor is not changed in the summer. She needs and deserves admiration – it is the element that contents her – and she will flirt, unseriously, with any man. Her shoulders were bare that night, her dress was cut to show the division of her breasts and to show her breasts when she leaned over the board to play. She kept losing and flirting and making her losses seem like a part of the flirtation. Chaddy was in the other room. She lost three games, and when the third game ended, she fell back on the sofa and, looking at me squarely, said something about going out on the dunes to settle the score. Lawrence heard her. I looked at Lawrence. He seemed shocked and gratified at the same time, as if he had suspected all along that we were not playing for anything so insubstantial as money. I may be wrong, of course, but I think that Lawrence felt that in watching our backgammon he was observing the progress of a mordant tragedy in which the money we won and lost served as a symbol for more vital forfeits. It is like Lawrence to try to read significance and finality into every gesture that we make, and it is certain of Lawrence that when he finds the inner logic to our conduct, it will be sordid.

Chaddy came in to play with me. Chaddy and I have never liked to lose to each other. When we were younger, we used to be forbidden to play games together, because they always ended in a fight. We think we know each other's mettle intimately. I think he is prudent; he thinks I am foolish. There is always bad blood when we play anything – tennis or backgammon or softball or bridge – and it does seem at times as if we were playing for the possession of each other's liberties. When I lose to Chaddy, I can't sleep. All this is only half the truth of our competitive relationship, but it was the half-truth that would be discernible to Lawrence, and his presence at the table made me so self-conscious that I lost two games. I tried not to seem angry when I got up from the board. Lawrence was watching me. I went out onto the terrace to suffer there in the dark the anger I always feel when I lose to Chaddy.

When I came back into the room, Chaddy and Mother were playing. Lawrence was still watching. By his lights, Odette had lost her virtue to me, I had lost my self-esteem to Chaddy, and now I wondered what he saw in the present match. He watched raptly, as if the opaque checkers and the marked board served for an exchange of critical power. How dramatic the board, in its ring of light, and the quiet players and the crash of the sea outside must have seemed to him! Here was spiritual cannibalism made visible; here, under his nose, were the symbols of the rapacious use human beings make of one another.

Mother plays a shrewd, an ardent, and an interfering game. She always has her hands in her opponent's board. When she plays with Chaddy, who is her favorite, she plays intently. Lawrence would have noticed this. Mother is a sentimental woman. Her heart is good and easily moved

by tears and frailty, a characteristic that, like her handsome nose, has not been changed at all by age. Grief in
another provokes her deeply, and she seems at times to be
trying to divine in Chaddy some grief, some loss, that she
can succor and redress, and so re-establish the relationship that she enjoyed with him when he was sickly and
young. She loves defending the weak and the childlike, and
now that we are old, she misses it. The world of debts
and business, men and war, hunting and fishing has on her
an exacerbating effect. (When Father drowned, she threw
away his fly rods and his guns.) She has lectured us all end-
lessly on self-reliance, but when we come back to her for
comfort and for help – particularly Chaddy – she seems to
feel most like herself. I suppose Lawrence thought that the
old woman and her son were playing for each other's soul.

She lost. 'Oh *dear*,' she said. She looked stricken and
bereaved, as she always does when she loses. 'Get me my
glasses, get me my checkbook, get me something to drink.'
Lawrence got up at last and stretched his legs. He looked
at us all bleakly. The wind and the sea had risen, and I
thought that if he heard the waves, he must hear them only
as a dark answer to all his dark questions; that he would
think that the tide had expunged the embers of our picnic
fires. The company of a lie is unbearable, and he seemed
like the embodiment of a lie. I couldn't explain to him the
simple and intense pleasures of playing for money, and it
seemed to me hideously wrong that he should have sat at
the edge of the board and concluded that we were playing

for one another's soul. He walked restlessly around the room two or three times and then, as usual, gave us a parting shot. 'I should think you'd go crazy,' he said, 'cooped up with one another like this, night after night. Come on, Ruth. I'm going to bed.'

THAT NIGHT, I dreamed about Lawrence. I saw his plain face magnified into ugliness, and when I woke in the morning, I felt sick, as if I had suffered a great spiritual loss while I slept, like the loss of courage and heart. It was foolish to let myself be troubled by my brother. I needed a vacation. I needed to relax. At school, we live in one of the dormitories, we eat at the house table, and we never get away. I not only teach English winter and summer but I work in the principal's office and fire the pistol at track meets. I needed to get away from this and from every other form of anxiety, and I decided to avoid my brother. Early that day, I took Helen and the children sailing, and we stayed out until suppertime. The next day, we went on a picnic. Then I had to go to New York for a day, and when I got back, there was the costume dance at the boat club. Lawrence wasn't going to this, and it's a party where I always have a wonderful time.

The invitations that year said to come as you wish you were. After several conversations, Helen and I had decided what to wear. The thing she most wanted to be again, she said, was a bride, and so she decided to wear her wedding dress. I thought this was a good choice – sincere, lighthearted, and inexpensive. Her choice influenced mine, and I decided to wear an old football uniform. Mother decided to go as Jenny Lind, because there was an old Jenny Lind costume in the attic. The others decided to rent costumes, and when I went to New York, I got the clothes. Lawrence and Ruth didn't enter into any of this.

Helen was on the dance committee, and she spent most of Friday decorating the club. Diana and Chaddy and I went sailing. Most of the sailing that I do these days is in Manhasset, and I am used to setting a homeward course by the gasoline barge and the tin roofs of the boat shed, and it was a pleasure that afternoon, as we returned, to keep the bow on a white church spire in the village and to find even the inshore water green and clear. At the end of our sail, we stopped at the club to get Helen. The committee had been trying to give a submarine appearance to the ballroom, and the fact that they had nearly succeeded in accomplishing this illusion made Helen very happy. We drove back to Laud's Head. It had been a brilliant afternoon, but on the way home we could smell the east wind – the dark wind, as Lawrence would have said – coming in from the sea.

My wife, Helen, is thirty-eight, and her hair would be gray, I guess, if it were not dyed, but it is dyed an unobtrusive yellow – a faded color – and I think it becomes her. I mixed cocktails that night while she was dressing, and when I took a glass upstairs to her, I saw her for the first time since our marriage in her wedding dress. There would be no point in saying that she looked to me more beautiful than she did on our wedding day, but because I have grown older and have, I think, a greater depth of feeling, and because I could see in her face that night both youth and age, both her devotion to the young woman that she had been and the positions that she had yielded graciously to time, I think I have never been so deeply moved. I had already put on the football uniform, and the weight of it, the heaviness of the pants and the shoulder guards, had worked a change in me, as if in putting on these old clothes I had put off the reasonable anxieties and troubles of my life. It felt as if we had both returned to the years before our marriage, the years before the war.

The Collards had a big dinner party before the dance, and our family – excepting Lawrence and Ruth – went to this. We drove over to the club, through the fog, at about half past nine. The orchestra was playing a waltz. While I was checking my raincoat, someone hit me on the back. It was Chucky Ewing, and the funny thing was that Chucky had on a football uniform. This seemed comical as hell to both of us. We were laughing when we went down the hall to the dance floor. I stopped at the door to look at the party, and it was beautiful. The committee had hung fish nets around the sides and over the high ceiling. The nets on the ceiling were filled with colored balloons. The light was soft and uneven, and the people – our friends and neighbors – dancing in the soft light to 'Three O'Clock in the Morning' made a pretty picture. Then I noticed the number of women dressed in white, and I realized that they, like Helen, were wearing wedding dresses. Patsy Hewitt and Mrs Gear and the Lackland girl waltzed by, dressed as brides. Then Pep Talcott came over to where Chucky and I were standing. He was dressed to be Henry VIII, but he told us that the Auerbach twins and Henry Barrett and Dwight MacGregor were all wearing football uniforms, and that by the last count there were ten brides on the floor.

This coincidence, this funny coincidence, kept everybody laughing, and made this one of the most lighthearted parties we've ever had at the club. At first I thought that the women had planned with one another to wear wedding dresses, but the ones that I danced with said it was a coincidence and I'm sure that Helen had made her decision alone. Everything went smoothly for me until a little before midnight. I saw Ruth standing at the edge of the floor. She was wearing a long red dress. It was all wrong. It wasn't the spirit of the party at all. I danced with her, but no one cut in, and I was darned if I'd spend the rest of the night dancing with her and I asked her where Lawrence was. She said he was out on the dock, and I took her over to the bar and left her and went out to get Lawrence.

The east fog was thick and wet, and he was alone on the dock. He was not in costume. He had not even bothered to get himself up as a fisherman or a sailor. He looked particularly saturnine. The fog blew around us like a cold smoke. I wished that it had been a clear night, because the easterly fog seemed to play into my misanthropic brother's hands. And I knew that the buoys – the groaners and bells that we could hear then – would sound to him like half-human, half-drowned cries, although every sailor knows that buoys are necessary and reliable fixtures, and I knew that the foghorn at the lighthouse would mean wanderings and losses to him and that he could misconstrue the vivacity of the dance music. 'Come on in, Tifty,' I said, 'and dance with your wife or get her some partners.'

'Why should I?' he said. 'Why should I?' And he walked to the window and looked in at the party. 'Look at it,' he said. 'Look at that . . .'

Chucky Ewing had got hold of a balloon and was trying to organize a scrimmage line in the middle of the floor. The others were dancing a samba. And I knew that Lawrence was looking bleakly at the party as he had looked at the weather-beaten shingles on our house, as if he saw here an abuse and a distortion of time; as if in wanting to be brides and football players we exposed the fact that, the lights of youth having been put out in us, we had been unable to find other lights to go by and, destitute of faith and principle, had become foolish and sad. And that he was thinking this about so many kind and happy and generous people made me angry, made me feel for him such an unnatural abhorrence that I was ashamed, for he is my brother and a Pommeroy. I put my arm around his shoulders and tried to force him to come in, but he wouldn't.

I got back in time for the Grand March, and after the

prizes had been given out for the best costumes, they let the balloons down. The room was hot, and someone opened the big doors onto the dock, and the easterly wind circled the room and went out, carrying across the dock and out onto the water most of the balloons. Chucky Ewing went running out after the balloons, and when he saw them pass the dock and settle on the water, he took off his football uniform and dove in. Then Eric Auerbach dove in and Lew Phillips dove in and I dove in, and you know how it is at a party after midnight when people start jumping into the water. We recovered most of the balloons and dried off and went on dancing, and we didn't get home until morning.

THE NEXT DAY was the day of the flower show. Mother and Helen and Odette all had entries. We had a pickup lunch, and Chaddy drove the women and children over to the show. I took a nap, and in the middle of the afternoon I got some trunks and a towel and, on leaving the house, passed Ruth in the laundry. She was washing clothes. I don't know why she should seem to have so much more work to do than anyone else, but she is always washing or ironing or mending clothes. She may have been taught, when she was young, to spend her time like this, or she may be at the mercy of an expiatory passion. She seems to scrub and iron with a penitential fervor, although I can't imagine what it is that she thinks she's done wrong. Her children were with her in the laundry. I offered to take them to the beach, but they didn't want to go.

It was late in August, and the wild grapes that grow pro-
fusely all over the island made the land wind smell of wine.
There is a little grove of holly at the end of the path, and
then you climb the dunes, where nothing grows but that
coarse grass. I could hear the sea, and I remember thinking
how Chaddy and I used to talk mystically about the sea.
When we were young, we had decided that we could never
live in the West because we would miss the sea. 'It is very
nice here,' we used to say politely when we visited people
in the mountains, 'but we miss the Atlantic.' We used to
look down our noses at people from Iowa and Colorado
who had been denied this revelation, and we scorned the
Pacific. Now I could hear the waves, whose heaviness
sounded like a reverberation, like a tumult, and it pleased
me as it had pleased me when I was young, and it seemed
to have a purgative force, as if it had cleared my memory
of, among other things, the penitential image of Ruth in
the laundry.

But Lawrence was on the beach. There he sat. I went in
without speaking. The water was cold, and when I came
out, I put on a shirt. I told him that I was going to walk up
to Tanners Point, and he said that he would come with me.
I tried to walk beside him. His legs are no longer than
mine, but he always likes to stay a little ahead of his com-
panion. Walking along behind him, looking at his bent
head and his shoulders, I wondered what he could make of
that landscape.

There were the dunes and cliffs, and then, where they

declined, there were some fields that had begun to turn from green to brown and yellow. The fields were used for pasturing sheep, and I guess Lawrence would have noticed that the soil was eroded and that the sheep would accelerate this decay. Beyond the fields there are a few coastal farms, with square and pleasant buildings, but Lawrence could have pointed out the hard lot of an island farmer. The sea, at our other side, was the open sea. We always tell guests that there, to the east, lies the coast of Portugal, and for Lawrence it would be an easy step from the coast of Portugal to the tyranny in Spain. The waves broke with a noise like a 'hurrah, hurrah, hurrah,' but to Lawrence they would say '*Vale, vale.*' I suppose it would have occurred to his baleful and incisive mind that the coast was terminal moraine, the edge of the prehistoric world, and it must have occurred to him that we walked along the edge of the known world in spirit as much as in fact. If he should otherwise have overlooked this, there were some Navy planes bombing an uninhabited island to remind him.

That beach is a vast and preternaturally clean and simple landscape. It is like a piece of the moon. The surf had pounded the floor solid, so it was easy walking, and everything left on the sand had been twice changed by the waves. There was the spine of a shell, a broomstick, part of a bottle and part of a brick, both of them milled and broken until they were nearly unrecognizable, and I suppose Lawrence's sad frame of mind – for he kept his head down – went from one broken thing to another. The company of his pessimism began to infuriate me, and I caught up with him and put a hand on his shoulder. 'It's only a summer day, Tifty,' I said. 'It's only a summer day. What's the matter? Don't you like it here?'

'I don't like it here,' he said blandly, without raising his eyes. 'I'm going to sell my equity in the house to Chaddy. I didn't expect to have a good time. The only reason I came back was to say goodbye.'

I let him get ahead again and I walked behind him, looking at his shoulders and thinking of all the goodbyes he had made. When Father drowned, he went to church and said goodbye to Father. It was only three years later that he concluded that Mother was frivolous and said goodbye to her. In his freshman year at college, he had been very good friends with his roommate, but the man drank too much, and at the beginning of the spring term Lawrence changed roommates and said goodbye to his friend. When he had been in college for two years, he concluded that the atmosphere was too sequestered and he said goodbye to Yale. He enrolled at Columbia and got his law degree there, but he found his first employer dishonest, and at the end of six months he said goodbye to a good job. He married Ruth in City Hall and said goodbye to the Protestant Episcopal Church; they went to live on a back street in Tuckahoe and said goodbye to the middle class. In 1938, he went to Washington to work as a government lawyer, saying goodbye to private enterprise, but after eight months in Washington he concluded that the Roosevelt administration was sentimental and he said goodbye to it. They left Washington for a suburb of Chicago, where he said goodbye to his neighbors, one by one, on counts of drunkenness, boorishness, and stupidity. He said goodbye to Chicago and went to Kansas; he said goodbye to Kansas and went to Cleveland. Now he had said goodbye to Cleveland and come East again, stopping at Laud's Head long enough to say goodbye to the sea.

It was elegiac and it was bigoted and narrow, it mistook circumspection for character, and I wanted to help him. 'Come out of it,' I said. 'Come out of it, Tifty.'

'Come out of what?'

'Come out of this gloominess. Come out of it. It's only a summer day. You're spoiling your own good time and you're spoiling everyone else's. We need a vacation, Tifty. I need one. I need to rest. We all do. And you've made everything tense and unpleasant. I only have two weeks in the year. Two weeks. I need to have a good time and so do all the others. We need to rest. You think that your pessimism is an advantage, but it's nothing but an unwillingness to grasp realities.'

'What are the realities?' he said. 'Diana is a foolish and a promiscuous woman. So is Odette. Mother is an alcoholic. If she doesn't discipline herself, she'll be in a hospital in a year or two. Chaddy is dishonest. He always has been. The house is going to fall into the sea.' He looked at me and added, as an afterthought, 'You're a fool.'

'You're a gloomy son of a bitch,' I said. 'You're a gloomy son of a bitch.'

'Get your fat face out of mine,' he said. He walked along.

Then I picked up a root and, coming at his back – although I have never hit a man from the back before – I swung the root, heavy with sea water, behind me, and the momentum sped my arm and I gave him, my brother, a blow on the head that forced him to his knees on the sand, and I saw the blood come out and begin to darken his hair. Then I wished that he was dead, dead and about to be buried, not buried but about to be buried, because I did not want to be denied ceremony and decorum in putting him away, in putting him out of my consciousness, and I saw the rest of us – Chaddy and Mother and Diana and Helen – in mourning in the house on Belvedere Street that was torn down twenty years ago, greeting our guests and our relatives at the door and answering their mannerly condolences with mannerly grief. Nothing decorous was lacking so that even if he had been murdered on a beach, one would feel before the tiresome ceremony ended that he had come into the winter of his life and that it was a law of nature, and a beautiful one, that Tifty should be buried in the cold, cold ground.

He was still on his knees. I looked up and down. No one had seen us. The naked beach, like a piece of the moon, reached to invisibility. The spill of a wave, in a glancing run, shot up to where he knelt. I would still have liked to end him, but now I had begun to act like two men, the murderer and the Samaritan. With a swift roar, like hollowness made sound, a white wave reached him and encircled him, boiling over his shoulders, and I held him against the undertow. Then I led him to a higher place. The blood had spread all through his hair, so that it looked black. I took off my shirt and tore it to bind up his head. He was conscious, and I didn't think he was badly hurt. He didn't speak. Neither did I. Then I left him there.

I walked a little way down the beach and turned to watch him, and I was thinking of my own skin then. He had got to his feet and he seemed steady. The daylight was still clear, but on the sea wind fumes of brine were blowing in like a light fog, and when I had walked a little way from him, I could hardly see his dark figure in this obscurity. All down the beach I could see the heavy salt air blowing in. Then I turned my back on him, and as I got near to the house, I went swimming again, as I seem to have done after every encounter with Lawrence that summer.

When I got back to the house, I lay down on the terrace. The others came back. I could hear Mother defaming the flower arrangements that had won prizes. None of ours had won anything. Then the house quieted, as it always does at that hour. The children went into the kitchen to get supper and the others went upstairs to bathe. Then I heard Chaddy making cocktails, and the conversation about the flower-show judges was resumed. Then Mother cried, 'Tifty! Tifty! Oh, Tifty!'

He stood in the door, looking half dead. He had taken off the bloody bandage and he held it in his hand. 'My brother did this,' he said. 'My brother did it. He hit me with a stone – something – on the beach.' His voice broke with self-pity. I thought he was going to cry. No one else spoke. 'Where's Ruth?' he cried. 'Where's Ruth? Where in hell is Ruth? I want her to start packing. I don't have any more time to waste here. I have important things to do. I have *important* things to do.' And he went up the stairs.

THEY LEFT FOR the mainland the next morning, taking the six o'clock boat. Mother got up to say goodbye, but she was the only one, and it is a harsh and an easy scene to imagine – the matriarch and the changeling, looking at each other with a dismay that would seem like the powers of love reversed. I heard the children's voices and the car go down the drive, and I got up and went to the window, and what a morning that was! Jesus, what a morning! The wind was northerly. The air was clear. In the early heat, the roses in the garden smelled like strawberry jam. While I was dressing, I heard the boat whistle, first the warning signal and then the double blast, and I could see the good people on the top deck drinking coffee out of fragile paper cups, and Lawrence at the bow, saying to the sea, '*Thalassa, thalassa*,' while his timid and unhappy children watched the creation from the encirclement of their mother's arms. The buoys would toll mournfully for Lawrence, and while the grace of the light would make it an exertion not to throw out your arms and swear exultantly, Lawrence's eyes would trace the black sea as it fell astern;

he would think of the bottom, dark and strange, where full fathom five our father lies.

Oh, what can you do with a man like that? What can you do? How can you dissuade his eye in a crowd from seeking out the cheek with acne, the infirm hand; how can you teach him to respond to the inestimable greatness of the race, the harsh surface beauty of life; how can you put his finger for him on the obdurate truths before which fear and horror are powerless? The sea that morning was iridescent and dark. My wife and my sister were swimming – Diana and Helen – and I saw their uncovered heads, black and gold in the dark water. I saw them come out and I saw that they were naked, unshy, beautiful, and full of grace, and I watched the naked women walk out of the sea.

Reunion

THE LAST TIME I saw my father was in Grand Central Station. I was going from my grandmother's in the Adirondacks to a cottage on the Cape that my mother had rented, and I wrote my father that I would be in New York between trains for an hour and a half, and asked if we could have lunch together. His secretary wrote to say that he would meet me at the information booth at noon, and at twelve o'clock sharp I saw him coming through the crowd. He was a stranger to me – my mother divorced him three years ago and I hadn't been with him since – but as soon as I saw him I felt that he was my father, my flesh and blood, my future and my doom. I knew that when I was grown I would be something like him; I would have to plan my campaigns within his limitations. He was a big, good-looking man, and I was terribly happy to see him again. He struck me on the back and shook my hand. 'Hi, Charlie,' he said. 'Hi, boy. I'd like to take you up to my club, but it's in the Sixties, and if you have to catch an early train I guess we'd better get something to eat around here.' He put his arm around me, and I smelled my father the way my mother sniffs a rose. It was a rich compound of whiskey, after-shave lotion, shoe polish, woolens, and the rankness of a mature male. I hoped that someone would see us together. I wished that we could be photographed. I wanted some record of our having been together.

We went out of the station and up a side street to a restaurant. It was still early, and the place was empty. The bartender was quarreling with a delivery boy, and there was one very old waiter in a red coat down by the kitchen door. We sat down, and my father hailed the waiter in a loud voice. '*Kellner!*' he shouted. '*Garçon! Cameriere! You!*' His boisterousness in the empty restaurant seemed out of place. 'Could we have a little service here!' he shouted. 'Chop-chop.' Then he clapped his hands. This caught the waiter's attention, and he shuffled over to our table.

'Were you clapping your hands at me?' he asked.

'Calm down, calm down, *sommelier*,' my father said. 'If it isn't too much to ask of you – if it wouldn't be too much above and beyond the call of duty, we would like a couple of Beefeater Gibsons.'

'I don't like to be clapped at,' the waiter said.

'I should have brought my whistle,' my father said. 'I have a whistle that is audible only to the ears of old waiters. Now, take out your little pad and your little pencil and see if you can get this straight: two Beefeater Gibsons. Repeat after me: two Beefeater Gibsons.'

'I think you'd better go somewhere else,' the waiter said quietly.

'That,' said my father, 'is one of the most brilliant suggestions I have ever heard. Come on, Charlie, let's get the hell out of here.'

I followed my father out of that restaurant into another. He was not so boisterous this time. Our drinks came, and he cross-questioned me about the baseball season. He then struck the edge of his empty glass with his knife and began shouting again. '*Garçon! Kellner! Cameriere! You!* Could we trouble you to bring us two more of the same.'

'How old is the boy?' the waiter asked.

'That,' my father said, 'is none of your God-damned business.'

'I'm sorry, sir,' the waiter said, 'but I won't serve the boy another drink.'

'Well, I have some news for you,' my father said. 'I have some very interesting news for you. This doesn't happen to be the only restaurant in New York. They've opened another on the corner. Come on, Charlie.'

He paid the bill, and I followed him out of that restaurant into another. Here the waiters wore pink jackets like hunting coats, and there was a lot of horse tack on the walls. We sat down, and my father began to shout again. 'Master of the hounds! Tallyhoo and all that sort of thing. We'd like a little something in the way of a stirrup cup. Namely, two Bibson Geefeaters.'

We'd like a little something in the way of a stirrup cup. Namely, two Bibson Geefeaters

'Two Bibson Geefeaters?' the waiter asked, smiling.

'You know damned well what I want,' my father said angrily. 'I want two Beefeater Gibsons, and make it snappy. Things have changed in jolly old England. So my friend the duke tells me. Let's see what England can produce in the way of a cocktail.'

'This isn't England,' the waiter said.

'Don't argue with me,' my father said. 'Just do as you're told.'

'I just thought you might like to know where you are,' the waiter said.

'If there is one thing I cannot tolerate,' my father said, 'it is an impudent domestic. Come on, Charlie.'

The fourth place we went to was Italian. '*Buon giorno,*' my father said. '*Per favore, possiamo avere due cocktail americani, forti, forti. Molto gin, poco vermut.*'

'I don't understand Italian,' the waiter said.

'Oh, come off it,' my father said. 'You understand Italian, and you know damned well you do. *Vogliamo due cocktail americani. Subito.*'

The waiter left us and spoke with the captain, who came over to our table and said, 'I'm sorry, sir, but this table is reserved.'

'All right,' my father said. 'Get us another table.'

'All the tables are reserved,' the captain said.

'I get it,' my father said. 'You don't desire our patronage. Is that it? Well, the hell with you. *Vada all' inferno.* Let's go, Charlie.'

'I have to get my train,' I said.

'I'm sorry, sonny,' my father said. 'I'm terribly sorry.' He put his arm around me and pressed me against him. 'I'll walk you back to the station. If there had only been time to go up to my club.'

'That's all right, Daddy,' I said.

'I'll get you a paper,' he said. 'I'll get you a paper to read on the train.'

Then he went up to a newsstand and said, 'Kind sir, will you be good enough to favor me with one of your God-damned, no-good, ten-cent afternoon papers?' The clerk turned away from him and stared at a magazine cover. 'Is it asking too much, kind sir,' my father said, 'is it asking too much for you to sell me one of your disgusting specimens of yellow journalism?'

'I have to go, Daddy,' I said. 'It's late.'

'Now, just wait a second, sonny,' he said. 'Just wait a second. I want to get a rise out of this chap.'

'Goodbye, Daddy,' I said, and I went down the stairs and got my train, and that was the last time I saw my father.

The Swimmer

IT WAS ONE of those midsummer Sundays when everyone sits around saying, 'I *drank* too much last night.' You might have heard it whispered by the parishioners leaving church, heard it from the lips of the priest himself, struggling with his cassock in the *vestiarium*, heard it from the golf links and the tennis courts, heard it from the wildlife preserve where the leader of the Audubon group was suffering from a terrible hangover. 'I *drank* too much,' said Donald Westerhazy. 'We all *drank* too much,' said Lucinda Merrill. 'It must have been the wine,' said Helen Westerhazy. 'I *drank* too much of that claret.'

This was at the edge of the Westerhazys' pool. The pool, fed by an artesian well with a high iron content, was a pale shade of green. It was a fine day. In the west there was a massive stand of cumulus cloud so like a city seen from a distance – from the bow of an approaching ship – that it might have had a name. Lisbon. Hackensack. The sun was hot. Neddy Merrill sat by the green water, one hand in it, one around a glass of gin. He was a slender man – he seemed to have the especial slenderness of youth – and while he was far from young he had slid down his banister that morning and given the bronze backside of Aphrodite on the hall table a smack, as he jogged toward the smell of coffee in his dining room. He might have been compared to a summer's day, particularly the last hours of one, and while he lacked a tennis racket or a sail bag the impression was definitely one of youth, sport, and clement weather. He had been swimming and now he was breathing deeply, stertorously as if he could gulp into his lungs the components of that moment, the heat of the sun, the intenseness of his pleasure. It all seemed to flow into his chest. His own house stood in Bullet Park, eight miles to the south, where his four beautiful daughters would have had their lunch and might be playing tennis. Then it occurred to him that by taking a dogleg to the southwest he could reach his home by water.

His life was not confining and the delight he took in this observation could not be explained by its suggestion of escape. He seemed to see, with a cartographer's eye, that string of swimming pools, that quasi-subterranean stream that curved across the county. He had made a discovery, a contribution to modern geography; he would name the stream Lucinda after his wife. He was not a practical joker nor was he a fool but he was determinedly original and had a vague and modest idea of himself as a legendary figure. The day was beautiful and it seemed to him that a long swim might enlarge and celebrate its beauty.

He took off a sweater that was hung over his shoulders and dove in. He had an inexplicable contempt for men who did not hurl themselves into pools. He swam a choppy crawl, breathing either with every stroke or every fourth stroke and counting somewhere well in the back of his mind the one-two one-two of a flutter kick. It was not a serviceable stroke for long distances but the domestication of swimming had saddled the sport with some customs and in his part of the world a crawl was customary. To be embraced and sustained by the light green water was less a pleasure, it seemed, than the resumption of a natural condition, and he would have liked to swim without trunks, but this was not possible, considering his project. He hoisted himself up on the far curb – he never used the ladder – and started across the lawn. When Lucinda asked where he was going he said he was going to swim home.

The only maps and charts he had to go by were remembered or imaginary but these were clear enough. First there were the Grahams, the Hammers, the Lears, the Howlands, and the Crosscups. He would cross Ditmar Street to the Bunkers and come, after a short portage, to the Levys, the Welchers, and the public pool in Lancaster. Then there were the Hallorans, the Sachses, the Biswangers, Shirley Adams, the Gilmartins, and the Clydes. The day was lovely, and that he lived in a world so generously supplied with water seemed like a clemency, a beneficence. His heart was high and he ran across the grass. Making his way home by

an uncommon route gave him the feeling that he was a pilgrim, an explorer, a man with a destiny, and he knew that
he would find friends all along the way; friends would line
the banks of the Lucinda River.

He went through a hedge that separated the Westerhazys' land from the Grahams', walked under some flowering
apple trees, passed the shed that housed their pump and
filter, and came out at the Grahams' pool. 'Why, Neddy,'
Mrs Graham said, 'what a marvelous surprise. I've been trying to get you on the phone all morning. Here, let me get
you a drink.' He saw then, like any explorer, that the hospit-
able customs and traditions of the natives would have to be
handled with diplomacy if he was ever going to reach his
destination. He did not want to mystify or seem rude to the
Grahams nor did he have the time to linger there. He swam
the length of their pool and joined them in the sun and was
rescued, a few minutes later, by the arrival of two carloads
of friends from Connecticut. During the uproarious reunions he was able to slip away. He went down by the front
of the Grahams' house, stepped over a thorny hedge, and
crossed a vacant lot to the Hammers'. Mrs Hammer, looking up from her roses, saw him swim by although she wasn't
quite sure who it was. The Lears heard him splashing past
the open windows of their living room. The Howlands and
the Crosscups were away. After leaving the Howlands' he
crossed Ditmar Street and started for the Bunkers', where
he could hear, even at that distance, the noise of a party.

The water refracted the sound of voices and laughter

and seemed to suspend it in midair. The Bunkers' pool was on a rise and he climbed some stairs to a terrace where twenty-five or thirty men and women were drinking. The only person in the water was Rusty Towers, who floated there on a rubber raft. Oh, how bonny and lush were the banks of the Lucinda River! Prosperous men and women gathered by the sapphire-colored waters while caterer's men in white coats passed them cold gin. Overhead a red de Haviland trainer was circling around and around and around in the sky with something like the glee of a child in a swing. Ned felt a passing affection for the scene, a tenderness for the gathering, as if it was something he might touch. In the distance he heard thunder. As soon as Enid Bunker saw him she began to scream: 'Oh, look who's here! What a marvelous surprise! When Lucinda said that you couldn't come I thought I'd *die*.' She made her way to him through the crowd, and when they had finished kissing she led him to the bar, a progress that was slowed by the fact that he stopped to kiss eight or ten other women and shake the hands of as many men. A smiling bartender he had seen at a hundred parties gave him a gin and tonic and he stood by the bar for a moment, anxious not to get stuck in any conversation that would delay his voyage. When he seemed about to be surrounded he dove in and swam close to the side to avoid colliding with Rusty's raft. At the far end of the pool he bypassed the Tomlinsons with a broad smile and jogged up the garden path. The gravel cut his feet but this was the only unpleasantness. The party was confined to the pool, and as he went toward the house he heard the brilliant, watery sound of voices fade, heard the noise of a radio from the Bunkers' kitchen, where someone was listening to a ball game. Sunday afternoon. He made his way through the parked cars and down the grassy border of their driveway to Alewives Lane. He did not want to be seen on the road in his bathing trunks but there was no traffic and he made the short distance to the Levys' driveway, marked with a PRIVATE PROPERTY sign and a green tube for *The New York Times*. All the doors and windows of the big house were open but there were no signs of life; not even a dog barked. He went around the side of the house to the pool and saw that the Levys had only recently left. Glasses and bottles and dishes of nuts were on a table at the deep end, where there was a bathhouse or gazebo, hung with Japanese lanterns. After swimming the pool he got himself a glass and poured a drink. It was his fourth or fifth drink and he had swum nearly half the length of the Lucinda River. He felt tired, clean, and pleased at that moment to be alone; pleased with everything.

It would storm. The stand of cumulus cloud – that city – had risen and darkened, and while he sat there he heard the percussiveness of thunder again. The de Haviland trainer was still circling overhead and it seemed to Ned that he could almost hear the pilot laugh with pleasure in the afternoon; but when there was another peal of thunder he took off for home. A train whistle blew and he wondered what time it had gotten to be. Four? Five? He thought of the provincial station at that hour, where a waiter, his tuxedo concealed by a raincoat, a dwarf with some flowers wrapped in newspaper, and a woman who had been crying would be waiting for the local. It was suddenly growing dark; it was that moment when the pin-headed birds seem to organize their song into some acute and knowledgeable recognition of the storm's approach. Then there was a fine noise of rushing water from the crown of an oak at his back, as if a spigot there had been turned. Then the noise of fountains came from the crowns of all the tall trees. Why did he love storms, what was the meaning of his excitement when the door sprang open and the rain wind fled rudely up the stairs, why had the simple task of shutting the windows of an old house seemed fitting and urgent, why did the first watery notes of a storm wind have for him the unmistakable sound of good news, cheer, glad tidings? Then there was an explosion, a smell of cordite, and rain lashed the Japanese lanterns that Mrs Levy had bought in Kyoto the year before last, or was it the year before that?

He stayed in the Levys' gazebo until the storm had passed. The rain had cooled the air and he shivered. The force of the wind had stripped a maple of its red and yellow leaves and scattered them over the grass and the water. Since it was midsummer the tree must be blighted, and yet he felt a peculiar sadness at this sign of autumn. He braced his shoulders, emptied his glass, and started for the Welchers' pool. This meant crossing the Lindleys' riding ring and he was surprised to find it overgrown with grass and all the jumps dismantled. He wondered if the Lindleys had sold their horses or gone away for the summer and put them out to board. He seemed to remember having heard something about the Lindleys and their horses but the memory was unclear. On he went, barefoot through the wet grass, to the Welchers', where he found their pool was dry.

This breach in his chain of water disappointed him absurdly, and he felt like some explorer who seeks a torrential headwater and finds a dead stream. He was disappointed and mystified. It was common enough to go away for the summer but no one ever drained his pool. The Welchers had definitely gone away. The pool furniture was folded, stacked, and covered with a tarpaulin. The bathhouse was locked. All the windows of the house were shut, and when he went around to the driveway in front he saw a FOR SALE sign nailed to a tree. When had he last heard from the Welchers – when, that is, had he and Lucinda last regretted an invitation to dine with them? It seemed only a week or so ago. Was his memory failing or had he so disciplined it in the repression of unpleasant facts that he had damaged his sense of the truth? Then in the distance he heard the sound of a tennis game. This cheered him, cleared away all his apprehensions and let him regard the overcast sky and the cold air with indifference. This was the day that Neddy Merrill swam across the county. That was the day! He started off then for his most difficult portage.

HAD YOU GONE for a Sunday afternoon ride that day you might have seen him, close to naked, standing on the shoulders of Route 424, waiting for a chance to cross. You might have wondered if he was the victim of foul play, had his car broken down, or was he merely a fool. Standing barefoot in the deposits of the highway – beer cans, rags, and blowout patches – exposed to all kinds of ridicule, he seemed pitiful. He had known when he started that this was a part of his journey – it had been on his maps – but confronted with the lines of traffic, worming through the summery light, he found himself unprepared. He was laughed at, jeered at, a beer can was thrown at him, and he had no dignity or humor to bring to the situation. He could have gone back, back to the Westerhazys', where Lucinda would still be sitting in the sun. He had signed nothing, vowed nothing, pledged nothing, not even to himself. Why, believing as he did, that all human obduracy was susceptible to common sense, was he unable to turn back? Why was he determined to complete his journey even if it meant putting his life in danger? At what point had this prank, this joke, this piece of horseplay become serious? He could not go back, he could not even recall with any clearness the green water at the Westerhazys', the sense of inhaling the day's components, the friendly and relaxed voices saying that they had *drunk* too much. In the space of an hour, more or less, he had covered a distance that made his return impossible.

An old man, tooling down the highway at fifteen miles

an hour, let him get to the middle of the road, where there was a grass divider. Here he was exposed to the ridicule of the northbound traffic, but after ten or fifteen minutes he was able to cross. From here he had only a short walk to the Recreation Center at the edge of the village of Lancaster, where there were some handball courts and a public pool.

The effect of the water on voices, the illusion of brilliance and suspense, was the same here as it had been at the Bunkers' but the sounds here were louder, harsher, and more shrill, and as soon as he entered the crowded enclosure he was confronted with regimentation. 'ALL SWIMMERS MUST TAKE A SHOWER BEFORE USING THE POOL. ALL SWIMMERS MUST USE THE FOOTBATH. ALL SWIMMERS MUST WEAR THEIR IDENTIFICATION DISKS.' He took a shower, washed his feet in a cloudy and bitter solution, and made his way to the edge of the water. It stank of chlorine and looked to him like a sink. A pair of lifeguards in a pair of towers blew police whistles at what seemed to be regular intervals and abused the swimmers through a public address system. Neddy remembered the sapphire water at the Bunkers' with longing and thought that he might contaminate himself – damage his own prosperousness and charm – by swimming in this murk, but he reminded himself that he was an explorer, a pilgrim, and that this was merely a stagnant bend in the Lucinda River. He dove, scowling with distaste, into the chlorine and had to swim with his head above water to avoid collisions, but even so he was bumped into, splashed, and jostled. When he got to the shallow end both lifeguards were shouting at him: 'Hey, you, you without the identification disk, get outa the water.' He did, but they had no way of pursuing him and he went through the reek of suntan oil and chlorine out through the hurricane fence and passed the handball courts. By crossing the road he entered the wooded part of the Halloran estate. The woods were not cleared and the footing was treacherous and difficult until he reached the lawn and the clipped beech hedge that encircled their pool.

The Hallorans were friends, an elderly couple of enormous wealth who seemed to bask in the suspicion that they might be Communists. They were zealous reformers but they were not Communists, and yet when they were accused, as they sometimes were, of subversion, it seemed to gratify and excite them. Their beech hedge was yellow and he guessed this had been blighted like the Levys' maple. He called hullo, hullo, to warn the Hallorans of his approach, to palliate his invasion of their privacy. The Hallorans, for reasons that had never been explained to him, did not wear bathing suits. No explanations were in order, really. Their nakedness was a detail in their uncompromising zeal for reform and he stepped politely out of his trunks before he went through the opening in the hedge.

Mrs Halloran, a stout woman with white hair and a serene face, was reading the *Times*. Mr Halloran was taking beech leaves out of the water with a scoop. They seemed

not surprised or displeased to see him. Their pool was perhaps the oldest in the country, a fieldstone rectangle, fed
by a brook. It had no filter or pump and its waters were the
opaque gold of the stream.

'I'm swimming across the county,' Ned said.

'Why, I didn't know one could,' exclaimed Mrs
Halloran.

'Well, I've made it from the Westerhazys',' Ned said.
'That must be about four miles.'

He left his trunks at the deep end, walked to the shallow
end, and swam this stretch. As he was pulling himself out
of the water he heard Mrs Halloran say, 'We've been *terribly* sorry to hear about all your misfortunes, Neddy.'

'My misfortunes?' Ned asked. 'I don't know what you
mean.'

'Why, we heard that you'd sold the house and that your
poor children . . .'

'I don't recall having sold the house,' Ned said, 'and the
girls are at home.'

'Yes,' Mrs Halloran sighed. 'Yes . . .' Her voice filled the
air with an unseasonable melancholy and Ned spoke
briskly. 'Thank you for the swim.'

'Well, have a nice trip,' said Mrs Halloran.

Beyond the hedge he pulled on his trunks and fastened
them. They were loose and he wondered if, during the
space of an afternoon, he could have lost some weight. He
was cold and he was tired and the naked Hallorans and
their dark water had depressed him. The swim was too

much for his strength but how could he have guessed this, sliding down the banister that morning and sitting in the Westerhazys' sun? His arms were lame. His legs felt rubbery and ached at the joints. The worst of it was the cold in his bones and the feeling that he might never be warm again. Leaves were falling down around him and he smelled wood smoke on the wind. Who would be burning wood at this time of year?

He needed a drink. Whiskey would warm him, pick him up, carry him through the last of his journey, refresh his feeling that it was original and valorous to swim across the county. Channel swimmers took brandy. He needed a stimulant. He crossed the lawn in front of the Hallorans' house and went down a little path to where they had built a house for their only daughter, Helen, and her husband, Eric Sachs. The Sachses' pool was small and he found Helen and her husband there.

'Oh, *Neddy*,' Helen said. 'Did you lunch at Mother's?'

'Not *really*,' Ned said. 'I *did* stop to see your parents.' This seemed to be explanation enough. 'I'm terribly sorry to break in on you like this but I've taken a chill and I wonder if you'd give me a drink.'

'Why, I'd *love* to,' Helen said, 'but there hasn't been anything in this house to drink since Eric's operation. That was three years ago.'

Was he losing his memory, had his gift for concealing painful facts let him forget that he had sold his house, that his children were in trouble, and that his friend had been ill? His eyes slipped from Eric's face to his abdomen, where he saw three pale, sutured scars, two of them at least a foot long. Gone was his navel, and what, Neddy thought, would the roving hand, bed-checking one's gifts at 3 A.M., make of a belly with no navel, no link to birth, this breach in the succession?

'I'm sure you can get a drink at the Biswangers',' Helen said. 'They're having an enormous do. You can hear it from here. Listen!'

She raised her head and from across the road, the lawns, the gardens, the woods, the fields, he heard again the brilliant noise of voices over water. 'Well, I'll get wet,' he said, still feeling that he had no freedom of choice about his means of travel. He dove into the Sachses' cold water and, gasping, close to drowning, made his way from one end of the pool to the other. 'Lucinda and I want *terribly* to see you,' he said over his shoulder, his face set toward the Biswangers'. 'We're sorry it's been so long and we'll call you *very* soon.'

He crossed some fields to the Biswangers' and the sounds of revelry there. They would be honored to give him a drink, they would be happy to give him a drink. The Biswangers invited him and Lucinda for dinner four times a year, six weeks in advance. They were always rebuffed and yet they continued to send out their invitations, unwilling to comprehend the rigid and undemocratic realities of their society. They were the sort of people who discussed the price of things at cocktails, exchanged market tips during dinner, and after dinner told dirty stories to mixed company. They did not belong to Neddy's set – they were not even on Lucinda's Christmas-card list. He went toward their pool with feelings of indifference, charity, and some unease, since it seemed to be getting dark and these were the longest days of the year. The party when he joined it was noisy and large. Grace Biswanger was the kind of hostess who asked the optometrist, the veterinarian, the real-estate dealer, and the dentist. No one was swimming and the twilight, reflected on the water of the pool, had a wintry gleam. There was a bar and he started for this. When Grace Biswanger saw him she came toward him, not affectionately as he had every right to expect, but bellicosely.

'Why, this party has everything,' she said loudly, 'including a gate crasher.'

She could not deal him a social blow – there was no question about this and he did not flinch. 'As a gate crasher,' he asked politely, 'do I rate a drink?'

'Suit yourself,' she said. 'You don't seem to pay much attention to invitations.'

She turned her back on him and joined some guests, and he went to the bar and ordered a whiskey. The bartender served him but he served him rudely. His was a world in which the caterer's men kept the social score, and to be rebuffed by a part-time barkeep meant that he had suffered some loss of social esteem. Or perhaps the man was new and uninformed. Then he heard Grace at his back say: 'They went for broke overnight – nothing but income – and he showed up drunk one Sunday and asked us to loan him five thousand dollars . . .' She was always talking about money. It was worse than eating your peas off a knife. He dove into the pool, swam its length and went away.

The next pool on his list, the last but two, belonged to his old mistress, Shirley Adams. If he had suffered any injuries at the Biswangers' they would be cured here. Love – sexual roughhouse in fact – was the supreme elixir, the pain killer, the brightly colored pill that would put the spring back into his step, the joy of life in his heart. They had had an affair last week, last month, last year. He couldn't remember. It was he who had broken it off, his was the upper hand, and he stepped through the gate of the wall that surrounded her pool with nothing so considered as self-confidence. It seemed in a way to be his pool, as the lover, particularly the illicit lover, enjoys the possessions of his mistress with an authority unknown to holy matrimony. She was there, her hair the color of brass, but her figure, at the edge of the lighted, cerulean water, excited in him no profound memories. It had been, he thought, a lighthearted affair, although she had wept when he broke it off. She seemed confused to see him and he wondered if she was still wounded. Would she, God forbid, weep again?

'What do you want?' she asked.

'I'm swimming across the county.'

'Good Christ. Will you ever grow up?'

'What's the matter?'

'If you've come here for money,' she said, 'I won't give you another cent.'

'You could give me a drink.'

'I could but I won't. I'm not alone.'

'Well, I'm on my way.'

He dove in and swam the pool, but when he tried to haul himself up onto the curb he found that the strength in his arms and shoulders had gone, and he paddled to the ladder and climbed out. Looking over his shoulder he saw, in the lighted bathhouse, a young man. Going out onto the dark lawn he smelled chrysanthemums or marigolds – some stubborn autumnal fragrance – on the night air, strong as gas. Looking overhead he saw that the stars had come out, but why should he seem to see Andromeda, Cepheus, and Cassiopeia? What had become of the con-stellations of midsummer? He began to cry.

It was probably the first time in his adult life that he had ever cried, certainly the first time in his life that he had ever felt so miserable, cold, tired, and bewildered. He could not understand the rudeness of the caterer's bar-keep or the rudeness of a mistress who had come to him on her knees and showered his trousers with tears. He had swam too long, he had been immersed too long, and his nose and his throat were sore from the water. What he needed then was a drink, some company, and some clean, dry clothes, and while he could have cut directly across the road to his home he went on to the Gilmartins' pool. Here,

He had swam too long, he had been immersed too long, and his nose and throat were sore

for the first time in his life, he did not dive but went down the steps into the icy water and swam a hobbled sidestroke that he might have learned as a youth. He staggered with fatigue on his way to the Clydes' and paddled the length of their pool, stopping again and again with his hand on the curb to rest. He climbed up the ladder and wondered if he had the strength to get home. He had done what he wanted, he had swum the county, but he was so stupefied with exhaustion that his triumph seemed vague. Stooped, holding on to the gateposts for support, he turned up the driveway of his own house.

The place was dark. Was it so late that they had all gone to bed? Had Lucinda stayed at the Westerhazys' for supper? Had the girls joined her there or gone someplace else? Hadn't they agreed, as they usually did on Sunday, to regret all their invitations and stay at home? He tried the garage doors to see what cars were in but the doors were locked and rust came off the handles onto his hands. Going toward the house, he saw that the force of the thunderstorm had knocked one of the rain gutters loose. It hung down over the front door like an umbrella rib, but it could be fixed in the morning. The house was locked, and he thought that the stupid cook or the stupid maid must have locked the place up until he remembered that it had been some time since they had employed a maid or a cook. He shouted, pounded on the door, tried to force it with his shoulder, and then, looking in at the windows, saw that the place was empty.

The Scarlet Moving Van

GOODBYE TO THE mortal boredom of distributing a skinny chicken to a family of seven and all the other rites of the hill towns. I don't mean the real hill towns – Assisi or Perugia or Saracinesco, perched on a three-thousand-foot crag, with walls the dispiriting gray of shirt cardboards and mustard lichen blooming on the crooked roofs. The land, in fact, was flat, the houses frame. This was in the eastern United States, and the kind of place where most of us live. It was the unincorporated township of B____, with a population of perhaps two hundred married couples, all of them with dogs and children, and many of them with servants; it resembled a hill town only in a manner of speaking, in that the ailing, the disheartened, and the poor could not ascend the steep moral path that formed is natural defense, and the moment any of the inhabitants became infected with unhappiness or discontent, they sensed the hopelessness of existing on such a high spiritual altitude, and went to live in the plain. Life was unprecedentedly comfortable and tranquil. B____ was exclusively for the felicitous. The housewives kissed their husbands tenderly in the morning and passionately at nightfall. In nearly every house there were love, graciousness, and high hopes. The schools were excellent, the roads were smooth, the drains and other services were ideal, and one spring evening at dusk an immense scarlet moving van with gold lettering on its sides came up the street and stopped in the front of the Marple house, which had been empty then for three months.

The gilt and scarlet of the van, bright even in the twilight, was an inspired attempt to disguise the true sorrowfulness of wandering. 'We Carry Loads and Part Loads to All Far-Distant Places,' said the gold letters on the sides, and this legend had the effect of a distant train whistle. Martha Folkestone, who lived next door, watched through a window as the portables of her new neighbors were carried across the porch. 'That looks like real Chippendale,' she said, 'although it's hard to tell in this light. They have two children. They seem like nice people. Oh, I wish there was something I could bring them to make them feel at home. Do you think they'd like flowers? I suppose we could ask them for a drink. Do you think they'd like a drink? Would you want to go over and ask them if they'd like a drink?'

Later, when the furniture was all indoors and the van had gone, Charlie Folkestone crossed the lawn between the two houses and introduced himself to Peaches and

Gee-Gee. This is what he saw. Peaches was peaches – blond and warm, with a low-cut dress and a luminous front. Gee-Gee had been a handsome man, and perhaps still was, although his yellow curls were thin. His face seemed both angelic and menacing. He had never (Charlie learned later) been a boxer, but his eyes were slightly squinted and his square, handsome forehead had the conformation of layers of scar tissue. You might have said that his look was thoughtful until you realized that he was not a thoughtful man. It was the earnest and contained look of those who are a little hard of hearing or a little stupid.

They would be delighted to have a drink. They would be right over. Peaches wanted to put on some lipstick and say good night to the children, and then they would be right over. They came right over, and what seemed to be an un-usually pleasant evening began. The Folkestones had been worried about who their new neighbors would be, and to find a couple as sympathetic as Gee-Gee and Peaches made them very high-spirited. Like everyone else, they loved to express an opinion about their neighbors, and Gee-Gee and Peaches were, naturally, interested. It was the beginning of a friendship, and the Folkestones over-looked their usual concern with time and sobriety. It got late – it was past midnight – and Charlie did not notice how much whiskey was being poured or that Gee-Gee seemed to be getting drunk. Gee-Gee became very quiet – he dropped out of the conversation – and then he suddenly interrupted Martha in a flat, unpleasant drawl.

'God, but you're stuffy people,' he said.

'Oh, no, Gee-Gee!' Peaches said. 'Not on our first night!'

'You've had too much to drink, Gee-Gee,' Charlie said.

'Like hell I have,' said Gee-Gee. He bent over and began to unlace his shoes. 'I haven't had half enough.'

'Please, Gee-Gee, please,' Peaches said.

'I have to teach them, honey,' Gee-Gee said. 'They've got to learn.'

Then he stood up and, with the cunning and dexterity of a drunk, got out of most of his clothing before anyone could stop him.

'Get out of here,' Charlie said.

'The pleasure's all mine, neighbor,' said Gee-Gee. He kicked over a hammered-brass umbrella stand on his way out the door.

'Oh, I'm frightfully sorry!' Peaches said. 'I feel terribly about this!'

'Don't worry, my dear,' Martha said. 'He's probably very tired, and we've all had too much to drink.'

'Oh, no,' Peaches said. 'It always happens. Everywhere. We've moved eight times in the last eight years, and there's never been anyone to say goodbye to us. Not a soul. Oh, he was a beautiful man when I first knew him! You never saw anyone so fine and strong and generous. They called him the Greek God at college. That's why he's called Gee-Gee. He was All-America twice, but he was never a money player – he always played straight out of his heart. Everybody loved him. Now it's all gone, but I tell myself that I once had the love of a good man. I don't think many women have known that kind of love. Oh, I wish he'd come back. I wish he'd be the way he was. The night before last, when we were packing up the dishes in the old house, he got drunk and I slapped him in the face, and I shouted at him, "Come back! Come back! Come back to me, Gee-Gee!" But he didn't listen. He didn't hear me. He doesn't hear anyone any more – not even the voices of his children. I ask myself every day what I've done to be punished so cruelly.'

'I'm sorry, my dear!' Martha said.

'You won't be around to say goodbye when we go,' Peaches said. 'We'll last a year. You wait and see. Some people have tender farewell parties, but even the garbage man in the last place was glad to see us go.' With a grace and resignation that transcended the ruined evening, she began to gather up the clothing that her husband had scattered on the rug. 'Each time we move, I think that the change will be good for him,' she said. 'When we got here tonight, it all looked so pretty and quiet that I thought he might change. Well, you don't have to ask us again. You know what it's like.'

A FEW DAYS or perhaps a week later, Charlie saw Gee-Gee on the station platform in the morning and saw how completely personable his neighbor was when he was sober. B_____ was not an easy place to conquer, but Gee-Gee seemed already to have won the affectionate respect of his neighbors. Charlie could see, as he watched him standing in the sun among the other commuters, that he would be asked to join everything. Gee-Gee greeted Charlie heartily, and there was no trace of the ugliness he had shown that night. Indeed, it was impossible to believe that this charming and handsome man had been so offensive. In the morning light, and surrounded by new friends, he seemed to challenge the memory. He seemed almost able to transfer the blame onto Charlie.

Arrangements for the social initiation of the new couple were unusually rapid and elaborate, and began with a dinner party at the Watermans'. Charlie was already at the party when Gee-Gee and Peaches came in, and they came in like royalty. Arm in arm, radiant and beautiful, they seemed, at the moment of their entrance, to make the evening. It was a large party, and Charlie hardly saw them until they went in to dinner. He sat close to Peaches, but Gee-Gee was at the other end of the table. They were halfway through dessert when Gee-Gee's flat and unpleasant drawl sounded, like a parade command, over the general conversation.

'What a God-damned bunch of stuffed shirts!' he said. 'Let's put a little vitality into the conversation, shall we?' He sprang onto the center of the table and began to sing a dirty song and dance a jig. Women screamed. Dishes were upset and broken. Dresses were ruined. Peaches pled to her wayward husband. The effect of this outrageous performance was to empty the dining room of everyone but Gee-Gee and Charlie.

'Get down off there, Gee-Gee,' Charlie said.

'I have to teach them,' Gee-Gee said. 'I've got to teach them.'

'You're not teaching anybody anything but the fact that you're rotten drunk.'

'They've got to learn,' Gee-Gee said. 'I've got to teach them.' He got down off the table, breaking a few more dishes, and wandered out into the kitchen, where he embraced the cook, and then went on out into the night.

ONE MIGHT HAVE thought that this was warning enough to a worldly community, but unusual amounts of forgiveness were extended to Gee-Gee. One liked him, and there was always the chance that he might not misbehave. There was always his charming figure in the morning light to confound his enemies, but it began to seem more and more like a lure that would let him into houses where he could break the crockery. Forgiveness was not what he wanted, and if he seemed to have failed at offending the sensibilities of his hostess he would increase and complicate his outrageousness. No one had ever seen anything like it. He undressed at the Bilkers'. At the Levys' he drop-kicked a bowl of soft cheese onto the ceiling. He danced the Highland fling in his underpants, set fire to wastebaskets, and swung on the Townsends' chandelier – that famous chandelier. Inside of six weeks, there was not a house in B_____ where he was welcome.

The Folkestones still saw him, of course – saw him in

You're not teaching anybody anything but the fact that you're rotten drunk

his garden in the evening and talked to him across the hedge. Charlie was greatly troubled at the spectacle of someone falling so swiftly from grace, and he would have liked to help. He and Martha talked with Peaches, but Peaches was without hope. She did not understand what had happened to her Adonis, and that was as far as her intelligence took her. Now and then some innocent stranger from the next town or perhaps some newcomer would be taken with Gee-Gee and ask him to dinner. The performance was always the same, the dishes were always broken. The Folkestones were neighbors – there was this ancient bond – and Charlie may have thought that he could save the man. When Gee-Gee and Peaches quarreled, sometimes she telephoned Charlie and asked his protection. He went there one summer evening after she had telephoned. The quarrel was over; Peaches was reading a comic book in the living room, and Gee-Gee was sitting at the dining-room table with a drink in his hand. Charlie stood over his friend.

'Gee-Gee.'

'Yes.'

'Will you go on the wagon?'

'No.'

'Will you go on the wagon if I go on the wagon?'

'No.'

'Will you go to a psychiatrist?'

'Why? I know myself. I only have to play it out.'

'Will you go to a psychiatrist if I go with you?'

'No.'

'Will you do anything to help yourself?'

'I have to teach them.' Then he threw back his head and sobbed, 'Oh, Jesus . . .'

Charlie turned away. It seemed, at that instant, that Gee-Gee had heard, from some wilderness of his own, the noise of a distant horn that prophesied the manner and the hour of his death. There seemed to be some tremendous validity to the drunken man. Folkestone felt an upheaval in his spirit. He felt he understood the drunken man's message; he had always sensed it. It was at the bottom of their friendship. Gee-Gee was an advocate for the lame, the diseased, the poor, for those who through no fault of their own live out their lives in misery and pain. To the happy and the wellborn and the rich he had this to say – that for all their affection, their comforts, and their privileges, they would not be spared the pangs of anger and lust and the agonies of death. He only meant for them to be prepared for the blow when the blow fell. But was it not possible to accept this truth without having him dance a jig in your living room? He spoke from some vision of the suffering in life, but was it necessary to suffer oneself in order to accept his message? It seemed so.

'Gee-Gee?' Charlie asked.

'Yes.'

'*What* are you trying to teach them?'

'You'll never know. You're too God-damned stuffy.'

———

THEY DIDN'T EVEN last a year. In November, someone made them a decent offer for the house and they sold it. The gold-and-scarlet moving van returned, and they crossed the state line, into the town of Y_____, where they bought another house. The Folkestones were glad to see them go. A well-behaved young couple took their place, and everything was as it had been. They were seldom remembered. But through a string of friends Charlie learned, the following winter, that Gee-Gee had broken his hip playing football a day or two before Christmas. This fact, for some reason, remained with him, and one Sunday afternoon when he had nothing much better to do he got Gee-Gee's telephone number from Information and called his old neighbor to say that he was coming over for a drink. Gee-Gee roared with enthusiasm and gave Charlie directions for getting to the house.

It was a long drive, and halfway there Charlie wondered why he had undertaken it. Y_____ was several cuts below B_____. The house was in a development, and the builder had not stopped at mere ugliness; he had constructed a community that looked, with its rectilinear windows, like a penal colony. The streets were named after universities – Princeton Street, Yale Street, Rutgers Street, and so forth. Only a few of the houses had been sold, and Gee-Gee's house was surrounded by empty dwellings. Charlie rang the bell and heard Gee-Gee shouting for him to come in. The house was a mess, and as he was taking his coat off, Gee-Gee came slowly down the hall half riding in a child's wagon, which he propelled by pushing a crutch. His right hip and leg were encased in a massive cast.

'Where's Peaches?' Charlie asked.

'She's in Nassau. She and the children went to Nassau for Christmas.'

'And left you alone?'

'I wanted them to go. I made them go. Nothing can be done for me. I get along all right on this wagon. When I'm hungry, I make a sandwich. I wanted them to go. I made them go. Peaches needed a vacation, and I like being alone. Come on into the living room and make me a drink. I can't get the ice trays out – that's about the only thing I can't do. I can shave and get into bed and so forth, but I can't get the ice trays out.'

Charlie got some ice. He was glad to have something to do. The image of Gee-Gee in his wagon had shocked him, and he felt a terrifying stillness over the place. Out of the kitchen window he could see row upon row of ugly, empty houses. He felt as if some hideous melodrama were approaching its climax. But in the living room Gee-Gee was his most charming, and his smile and his voice gave the afternoon a momentary equilibrium. Charlie asked if Gee-Gee couldn't get a nurse to stay with him. Couldn't someone be found to stay with him? Couldn't he at least rent a wheelchair? Gee-Gee laughed away all these suggestions. He was contented. Peaches had written him from Nassau. They were having a marvelous time.

Charlie believed that Gee-Gee had made them go. It

was this detail, above everything else, that gave the situation its horror. Peaches would have liked, naturally enough, to go to Nassau, but she never would have insisted. She was much too innocent to have any envious dreams of travel. Gee-Gee would have insisted that she go; he would have made the trip so tempting that she could not, in her innocence, resist it. Did he wish to be left alone, drunken and crippled, in an isolated house? Did he need to feel abused? It seemed so. The disorder of the house and the image of his wife and children running, running, running on some coral beach seemed like a successful contrivance – a kind of triumph.

Gee-Gee lit a cigarette and, forgetting about it, lit another, and fumbled so clumsily with the matches that Charlie saw that he might easily burn to death. Hoisting himself from the wagon to the chair, he nearly fell, and, if he were alone and fell, he could easily die of hunger and thirst on his own rug. But there might be some drunken cunning in his clumsiness, his playing with fire. He smiled slyly when he saw the look on Charlie's face. 'Don't worry about me,' he said. 'I'll be all right. I have my guardian angel.'

'That's what everybody thinks,' Charlie said.

'Oh, but I have.'

Outside, it had begun to snow. The winter sky was overcast, and it would soon be dark. Charlie said that he had to go. 'Sit down,' Gee-Gee said. 'Sit down and have another drink.' Charlie's conscience held him there a few moments longer. How could he openly abandon a friend – a neighbor, at least – to the peril of death? But he had no choice; his family was waiting and he had to go. 'Don't worry about me,' Gee-Gee said when Charlie was putting on his coat. 'I have my angel.'

It was later than Charlie had realized. The snow was heavy now, and he had a two-hour drive, on winding back roads. There was a little rise going out of Y_____, and the new snow was so slick that he had trouble making the hill. There were steeper hills ahead of him. Only one of his windshield wipers worked, and the snow quickly covered the glass and left him with one small aperture onto the world. The snow sped into the headlights at a dizzying rate, and at one place where the road was narrow the car slid off onto the shoulder and he had to race the motor for ten minutes in order to get back onto the hard surface. It was a lonely stretch there – miles from any house – and he would have had a sloppy walk in his loafers. The car skidded and weaved up every hill, and it seemed that he reached the top by the thinnest margin of luck.

After driving for two hours, he was still far from home. The snow was so deep that guiding the car was like the trickiest kind of navigation. It took him three hours to get back, and he was tired when he drove into the darkness and peace of his own garage – tired and infinitely grateful. Martha and the children had eaten their supper, and she wanted to go over to the Lissoms' and discuss some school-board business. He told her that the driving was bad, and since it was such a short distance, she decided to walk. He lit a fire and made a drink, and the children sat at the table with him while he ate his supper. After supper on Sunday nights, the Folkestones played, or tried to play, trios. Charlie played the clarinet, his daughter played the piano, and his older son had a tenor recorder. The baby wandered around underfoot. This Sunday night they played simple arrangements of eighteenth-century music in the pleasantest family atmosphere – complimenting themselves when they squeezed through a difficult passage, and extending into the music what was best in their relationship. They were playing a Vivaldi sonata when the telephone rang. Charlie knew immediately who it was.

'Charlie, Charlie,' Gee-Gee said. 'Jesus. I'm in hot water. Right after you left I fell out of the God-damned wagon. It took me two hours to get to the telephone. You've got to get over. There's nobody else. You're my only friend. You've got to get over here. Charlie? You hear me?'

It must have been the strangeness of the look on Charlie's face that made the baby scream. The little girl picked him up in her arms, and stared, as did the other boy, at their father. They seemed to know the whole picture, every detail of it, and they looked at him calmly, as if they were expecting him to make some decision that had nothing to do with the continuing of a pleasant evening in a snowbound house – but a decision that would have a profound effect on their knowledge of him and on their final happiness. Their looks were, he thought, clear and appealing, and whatever he did would be final.

'You hear me, Charlie? You hear me?' Gee-Gee asked. 'It took me damned near two hours to crawl over to the telephone. You've got to help me. No one else will come.'

Charlie hung up. Gee-Gee must have heard the sound of his breathing and the baby crying, but Charlie had said nothing. He gave no explanation to the children, and they asked for none. They knew. His daughter went back to the piano, and when the telephone rang again and he did not answer it, no one questioned the ringing of the phone. They seemed happy and relieved when it stopped ringing, and they played Vivaldi until nine o'clock, when he sent them up to bed.

He made a drink to diminish the feeling that some emotional explosion had taken place, that some violence had shaken the air. He did not know what he had done or how to cope with his conscience. He would tell Martha about it when she came in, he thought. That would be a step toward comprehension. But when she returned he said nothing. He was afraid that if she brought her intelligence to the problem it would only confirm his guilt. 'But why didn't you telephone me at the Lissoms'?' she might have asked. 'I could have come home and you could have gone over.' She was too compassionate a woman to accept passively, as he was doing, the thought of a friend, a neighbor, lying in agony. She went on upstairs. He poured some whiskey into his glass. If he had called the Lissoms', if she had returned to care for the children and left him free to help Gee-Gee, would he have been able to make the return trip in the heavy snow? He could have put on chains, but where were the chains? Were they in the car or in the cellar? He didn't know. He hadn't used them that year. But perhaps by now the roads would have been plowed. Perhaps the storm was over. This last, distressing possibility made him feel sick. Had the sky betrayed him? He switched on the outside light and went hesitantly, unwillingly, toward the window.

The clean snow gave off an ingratiating sparkle, and the beam of light shone into empty and peaceful air. The snow must have stopped a few minutes after he had entered the house. But how could he have known? How could he be expected to take into consideration the caprices of the weather? And what about that look the children had given him – so stern, so clear, so like a declaration that his place at that hour was with them, and not with the succoring of drunkards who had forfeited the chance to be taken seriously?

Then the image of Gee-Gee returned, crushing in its misery, and he remembered Peaches standing in the hallway at the Watermans' calling, 'Come back! Come back!' She was calling back the youth that Charlie had never known, but it was easy to imagine what Gee-Gee must have been – fair, high-spirited, generous, and strong – and why had it all come to ruin? *Come back! Come back!* She seemed to call after the sweetness of a summer's day – roses in bloom and all the doors and windows open on the garden. It was all there in her voice; it was like the illusion of an abandoned house in the last rays of the sun. A large place, falling to pieces, haunted for children and a headache for the police and fire departments, but, seeing it with its windows blazing in the sunset, one thinks that they have all come back. Cook is in the kitchen rolling pastry. The smell of chicken rises up the back stairs. The front rooms are ready for the children and their many friends. A coal fire burns in the grate. Then as the light goes off the windows, the true ugliness of the place scowls into the dusk with redoubled force, as, when the notes of that long-ago summer left Peaches' voice, one saw the finality and confusion of despair in her innocent face. *Come back! Come back!* He poured himself some more whiskey, and as he raised the glass to his mouth he heard the wind change and saw – the outside light was still on – the snow begin to spin down again, with the vindictive swirl of a blizzard. The road was impassable; he could not have made the trip. The change in the weather had given him sweet absolution, and he watched the snow with a smile of love, but he stayed up until three in the morning with the bottle.

He was red-eyed and shaken the next morning, and ducked out of his office at eleven and drank two Martinis. He had two more before lunch and another at four and two on the train, and came reeling home for supper. The clinical details of heavy drinking are familiar to all of us; it is only the human picture that concerns us here, and Martha was finally driven to speak to him. She spoke most gently.

'You're drinking too much, darling,' she said. 'You've been drinking too much for three weeks.'

'My drinking,' he said, 'is my own God-damned business. You mind your business and I'll mind mine.'

It got worse and worse, and she had to do something. She finally went to their rector – a good-looking young bachelor who practiced both psychology and liturgy – for advice. He listened sympathetically. 'I stopped at the rectory this afternoon,' she said when she got home that night, 'and I talked with Father Hemming. He wonders why you haven't been in church, and he wants to talk to you. He's such a good-looking man,' she added, trying to make what she had just said sound less like a planned speech, 'that I wonder why he's never married.' Charlie – drunk, as usual – went to the telephone and called the rectory. 'Look, Father,' he said. 'My wife tells me that you've been entertaining her in the afternoons. Well, I don't like it. You keep your hands off my wife. You hear me? That damned black suit you wear doesn't cut any ice with me. You keep your hands off my wife or I'll bust your pretty little nose.'

In the end, he lost his job, and they had to move, and began their wanderings, like Gee-Gee and Peaches, in the scarlet-and-gold van.

AND WHAT HAPPENED to Gee-Gee – what ever became of him? That boozy guardian angel, her hair disheveled and the strings of her harp broken, still seemed to hover over where he lay. After telephoning Charlie that night, he telephoned the fire department. They were there in eight minutes flat, with bells ringing and sirens blowing. They got him into bed, made him a fresh drink, and one of the firemen, who had nothing better to do, stayed on until Peaches got back from Nassau. They had a fine time, eating all the steaks in the deep freeze and drinking a quart of bourbon every day. Gee-Gee could walk by the time Peaches and the children got back, and he took up that disorderly life for which he seemed so much better equipped than his neighbor, but they had to move at the end of the year, and, like the Folkestones, vanished from the hill towns.

O Youth and Beauty!

AT THE TAG end of nearly every long, large Saturday-night party in the suburb of Shady Hill, when almost everybody who was going to play golf or tennis in the morning had gone home hours ago and the ten or twelve people remaining seemed powerless to bring the evening to an end although the gin and whiskey were running low, and here and there a woman who was sitting out her husband would have begun to drink milk; when everybody had lost track of time, and the baby-sitters who were waiting at home for these diehards would have long since stretched out on the sofa and fallen into a deep sleep, to dream about cooking-contest prizes, ocean voyages, and romance; when the bellicose drunk, the crapshooter, the pianist, and the woman faced with the expiration of her hopes had all expressed themselves; when every proposal – to go to the Farquarsons' for breakfast, to go swimming, to go and wake up the Townsends, to go here and go there – died as soon as it was made, then Trace Bearden would begin to chide Cash Bentley about his age and thinning hair. The chiding was preliminary to moving the living-room furniture. Trace and Cash moved the tables and the chairs, the sofas and the fire screen, the woodbox and the footstool; and when they had finished, you wouldn't know the place. Then if the host had a revolver, he would be asked to produce it. Cash would take off his shoes and assume a starting crouch behind a sofa. Trace would fire the weapon out of an open window, and if you were new to the community and had not understood what the preparations were about, you would then realize that you were watching a hurdle race. Over the sofa went Cash, over the tables, over the fire screen and the woodbox. It was not exactly a race, since Cash ran it alone, but it was extraordinary to see this man of forty surmount so many obstacles so gracefully. There was not a piece of furniture in Shady Hill that Cash could not take in his stride. The race ended with cheers, and presently the party would break up.

Cash was, of course, an old track star, but he was never aggressive or tiresome about his brilliant past. The college where he had spent his youth had offered him a paying job on the alumni council, but he had refused it, realizing that that part of his life was ended. Cash and his wife, Louise, had two children, and they lived in a medium-cost ranch house on Alewives Lane. They belonged to the country club, although they could not afford it, but in the case of the Bentleys nobody ever pointed this out, and Cash was one of the best-liked men in Shady Hill. He was still slender – he was careful about his weight – and he walked to the train in the morning with a light and vigorous step that marked him as an athlete. His hair was thin, and there were mornings when his eyes looked bloodshot, but this did not detract much from a charming quality of stubborn youthfulness.

In business Cash had suffered reverses and disappointments, and the Bentleys had many money worries. They were always late with their tax payments and their mortgage payments, and the drawer of the hall table was stuffed with unpaid bills; it was always touch and go with the Bentleys and the bank. Louise looked pretty enough on Saturday night, but her life was exacting and monotonous. In the pockets of her suits, coats, and dresses there were little wads and scraps of paper on which was written: 'Oleomargarine, frozen spinach, Kleenex, dog biscuit, hamburger, pepper, lard . . .' When she was still half awake in the morning, she was putting on the water for coffee and diluting the frozen orange juice. Then she would be wanted by the children. She would crawl under the bureau on her hands and knees to find a sock for Toby. She would lie flat on her belly and wiggle under the bed (getting dust up her nose) to find a shoe for Rachel. Then there were the housework, the laundry, and the cooking, as well as the demands of the children. There always seemed to be shoes to put on and shoes to take off, snowsuits to be zipped and unzipped, bottoms to be wiped, tears to be dried, and when the sun went down (she saw it set from the kitchen window) there was the supper to be cooked, the baths, the bedtime story, and the Lord's Prayer. With the sonorous words of the Our Father in a darkened room the children's day was over, but the day was far from over for Louise Bentley. There were the darning, the mending, and some ironing to do, and after sixteen years of housework she did not seem able to escape her chores even while she slept. Snowsuits, shoes, baths, and groceries seemed to have permeated her subconscious. Now and then she would speak in her sleep – so loudly that she woke her husband. 'I can't *afford* veal cutlets,' she said one night. Then she sighed uneasily and was quiet again.

By the standards of Shady Hill, the Bentleys were a happily married couple, but they had their ups and downs. Cash could be very touchy at times. When he came home after a bad day at the office and found that Louise, for some good reason, had not started supper, he would be ugly. 'Oh, for Christ sake!' he would say, and go into the kitchen and heat up some frozen food. He drank some whiskey to relax himself during this ordeal, but it never seemed to relax him, and he usually burned the bottom out of a pan, and when they sat down for supper the dining space would be full of smoke. It was only a question of time before they were plunged into a bitter quarrel. Louise would run upstairs, throw herself onto the bed and sob. Cash would grab the whiskey bottle and dose himself. These rows, in spite of the vigor with which Cash and Louise entered into them, were the source of a great deal of pain for both of them. Cash would sleep downstairs on the sofa, but sleep never repaired the damage, once the trouble had begun, and if they met in the morning, they would be at one another's throats in a second. Then Cash would leave for the train, and, as soon as the children had been taken to nursery school, Louise would put on her coat and cross the grass to the Beardens' house. She would cry into a cup of warmed-up coffee and tell Lucy Bearden her troubles. What was the meaning of marriage? What was the meaning of love? Lucy always suggested that Louise get a job. It would give her emotional and financial independence, and that, Lucy said, was what she needed.

The next night, things would get worse. Cash would not come home for dinner at all, but would stumble in at about eleven, and the whole sordid wrangle would be repeated, with Louise going to bed in tears upstairs and Cash again stretching out on the living-room sofa. After a few days and nights of this, Louise would decide that she was at the end of her rope. She would decide to go and stay with her married sister in Mamaroneck. She usually chose a Saturday, when Cash would be at home, for her departure. She would pack a suitcase and get her War Bonds from the desk. Then she would take a bath and put on her best slip. Cash, passing the bedroom door, would see her. Her slip was transparent, and suddenly he was all repentance, tenderness, charm, wisdom, and love. 'Oh, my darling!' he would groan, and when they went downstairs to get a bite to eat about an hour later, they would be sighing and making cow eyes at one another; they would be the happiest married couple in the whole eastern United States. It was usually at about this time that Lucy Bearden turned up with the good news that she had found a job for Louise. Lucy would ring the doorbell, and Cash, wearing a bathrobe, would let her in. She would be brief with Cash, naturally, and hurry into the dining room to tell poor Louise the good news. 'Well, that's very nice of you to have looked,' Louise would say wanly, 'but I don't think that I want a job any more. I don't think that Cash wants me to work, do you, sweetheart?' Then she would turn her big dark eyes on Cash, and you could practically smell smoke. Lucy would excuse herself hurriedly from this scene of depravity, but never left with any hard feelings, because she had been married for nineteen years herself and she knew that every union has its ups and downs. She didn't seem to leave any wiser, either; the next time the Bentleys quarreled she would be just as intent as ever on getting Louise a job. But these quarrels and reunions, like the hurdle race, didn't seem to lose their interest through repetition.

ON A SATURDAY night in the spring, the Farquarsons gave the Bentleys an anniversary party. It was their seventeenth anniversary. Saturday afternoon, Louise Bentley put herself through preparations nearly as arduous as the Monday wash. She rested for an hour, by the clock, with her feet high in the air, her chin in a sling, and her eyes bathed in

some astringent solution. The clay packs, the too tight gir-
dle, and the plucking and curling and painting that went
on were all aimed at rejuvenation. Feeling in the end that
she had not been entirely successful, she tied a piece of
veiling over her eyes – but she was a lovely woman, and all
the cosmetics that she had struggled with seemed, like her
veil, to be drawn transparently over a face where mature
beauty and a capacity for wit and passion were undisguis-
able. The Farquarsons' party was nifty, and the Bentleys
had a wonderful time. The only person who drank too
much was Trace Bearden. Late in the party, he began to
chide Cash about his thinning hair and Cash good-
naturedly began to move the furniture around. Harry
Farquarson had a pistol, and Trace went out onto the terrace to fire it up at the sky. Over the sofa went Cash, over
the end table, over the arms of the wing chair and the fire
screen. It was a piece of carving on a chest that brought
him down, and down he came like a ton of bricks.

Louise screamed and ran to where he lay. He had cut a
gash in his forehead, and someone made a bandage to stop
the flow of blood. When he tried to get up, he stumbled
and fell again, and his face turned a terrible green. Harry
telephoned Dr Parminter, Dr Hopewell, Dr Altman, and Dr
Barnstable, but it was two in the morning and none of
them answered. Finally, a Dr Yerkes – a total stranger –
agreed to come. Yerkes was a young man – he did not seem
old enough to be a doctor – and he looked around at the
disordered room and the anxious company as if there was

something weird about the scene. He got off on the wrong foot with Cash. 'What seems to be the matter, old-timer?' he asked.

Cash's leg was broken. The doctor put a splint on it, and Harry and Trace carried the injured man out to the doctor's car. Louise followed them in her own car to the hospital, where Cash was bedded down in a ward. The doctor gave Cash a sedative, and Louise kissed him and drove home in the dawn.

CASH WAS IN the hospital for two weeks, and when he came home he walked with a crutch and his broken leg was in a heavy cast. It was another ten days before he could limp to the morning train. 'I won't be able to run the hurdle race any more, sweetheart,' he told Louise sadly. She said that it didn't matter, but while it didn't matter to her, it seemed to matter to Cash. He had lost weight in the hospital. His spirits were low. He seemed discontented. He did not himself understand what had happened. He, or everything around him, seemed subtly to have changed for the worse. Even his senses seemed to conspire to damage the ingenuous world that he had enjoyed for so many years. He went into the kitchen late one night to make himself a sandwich, and when he opened the icebox door he noticed a rank smell. He dumped the spoiled meat into the garbage, but the smell clung to his nostrils. A few days later he was in the attic, looking for his varsity sweater. There were no windows in the attic and his flashlight was dim. Kneeling on the floor to unlock a trunk, he broke a spider web with his lips. The frail web covered his mouth as if a hand had been put over it. He wiped it impatiently, but also with the feeling of having been gagged. A few nights later, he was walking down a New York side street in the rain and saw an old whore standing in a doorway. She was so sluttish and ugly that she looked like a cartoon of Death, but before he could appraise her – the instant his eyes took an impression of her crooked figure – his lips swelled, his breathing quickened, and he experienced all the other symptoms of erotic excitement. A few nights later, while he was reading *Time* in the living room, he noticed that the faded roses Louise had brought in from the garden smelled more of earth than of anything else. It was a putrid, compelling smell. He dropped the roses into a wastebasket, but not before they had reminded him of the spoiled meat, the whore, and the spider web.

He had started going to parties again, but without the hurdle race to run, the parties of his friends and neighbors seemed to him interminable and stale. He listened to their dirty jokes with an irritability that was hard for him to conceal. Even their countenances discouraged him, and, slumped in a chair, he could regard their skin and their teeth narrowly, as if he were himself a much younger man.

The brunt of his irritability fell on Louise, and it seemed to her that Cash, in losing the hurdle race, had lost the thing that had preserved his equilibrium. He was rude to his friends when they stopped in for a drink. He was rude and gloomy when he and Louise went out. When Louise asked him what was the matter, he only murmured, 'Nothing, nothing, nothing,' and poured himself some bourbon. May and June passed, and then the first part of July, without his showing any improvement.

THEN IT IS a summer night, a wonderful summer night. The passengers on the eight-fifteen see Shady Hill – if they notice it at all – in a bath of placid golden light. The noise of the train is muffled in the heavy foliage, and the long car windows look like a string of lighted aquarium tanks before they flicker out of sight. Up on the hill, the ladies say to one another, 'Smell the grass! Smell the trees!' The Farquarsons are giving another party, and Harry has hung a sign, WHISKEY GULCH, from the rose arbor, and is wearing a chef's white hat and an apron. His guests are still drinking, and the smoke from his meat fire rises, on this windless evening, straight up into the trees.

In the clubhouse on the hill, the first of the formal dances for the young people begins around nine. On Alewives Lane sprinklers continue to play after dark. You can smell the water. The air seems as fragrant as it is dark – it is a delicious element to walk through – and most of the windows on Alewives Lane are open to it. You can see Mr and Mrs Bearden, as you pass, looking at their television. Joe Lockwood, the young lawyer who lives on the corner, is practicing a speech to the jury before his wife. 'I intend to show you,' he says, 'that a man of probity, a man whose reputation for honesty and reliability . . .' He waves his bare arms as he speaks. His wife goes on knitting. Mrs Carver – Harry Farquarson's mother-in-law – glances up at the sky and asks, '*Where* did all the stars come from?' She is old and foolish, and yet she is right: Last night's stars seem to have drawn to themselves a new range of galaxies, and the night sky is not dark at all, except where there is a tear in the membrane of light. In the unsold house lots near the track a hermit thrush is singing.

The Bentleys are at home. Poor Cash has been so rude and gloomy that the Farquarsons have not asked him to their party. He sits on the sofa beside Louise, who is sewing elastic into the children's underpants. Through the open window he can hear the pleasant sounds of the summer night. There is another party, in the Rogerses' garden, behind the Bentleys'. The music from the dance drifts down the hill. The band is sketchy – saxophone, drums, and piano – and all the selections are twenty years old. The band plays 'Valencia,' and Cash looks tenderly toward Louise, but Louise, tonight, is a discouraging figure. The lamp picks out the gray in her hair. Her apron is stained. Her face seems colorless and drawn. Suddenly, Cash begins frenziedly to beat his feet in time to the music. He sings some gibberish – Jabajabajabajaba – to the distant saxophone. He sighs and goes into the kitchen.

Here a faint, stale smell of cooking clings to the dark. From the kitchen window Cash can see the lights and figures of the Rogerses' party. It is a young people's party.

The Rogers girl has asked some friends in for dinner before the dance, and now they seem to be leaving. Cars are driving away. 'I'm covered with grass stains,' a girl says. 'I hope the old man remembered to buy gasoline,' a boy says, and a girl laughs. There is nothing on their minds but the passing summer nights. Taxes and the elastic in underpants – all the unbeautiful facts of life that threaten to crush the breath out of Cash – have not touched a single figure in this garden. Then jealousy seizes him – such savage and bitter jealousy that he feels ill.

He does not understand what separates him from these children in the garden next door. He has been a young man. He has been a hero. He has been adored and happy and full of animal spirits, and now he stands in a dark kitchen, deprived of his athletic prowess, his impetuousness, his good looks – of everything that means anything to him. He feels as if the figures in the next yard are the specters from some party in that past where all his tastes and desires lie, and from which he has been cruelly removed. He feels like a ghost of the summer evening. He is sick with longing. Then he hears voices in the front of the house. Louise turns on the kitchen light. 'Oh, here you are,' she says. 'The Beardens stopped in. I think they'd like a drink.'

Cash went to the front of the house to greet the Beardens. They wanted to go up to the club, for one dance. They saw, at a glance, that Cash was at loose ends, and they urged the Bentleys to come. Louise got someone to stay with the children and then went upstairs to change.

When they got to the club, they found a few friends of their age hanging around the bar, but Cash did not stay in the bar. He seemed restless and perhaps drunk. He banged into a table on his way through the lounge to the ballroom. He cut in on a young girl. He seized her too vehemently and jigged her off in an ancient two-step. She signaled openly for help to a boy in the stag line, and Cash was cut out. He walked angrily off the dance floor onto the terrace. Some young couples there withdrew from one another's arms as he pushed open the screen door. He walked to the end of the terrace, where he hoped to be alone, but here he surprised another young couple, who got up from the lawn, where they seemed to have been lying, and walked off in the dark toward the pool.

Louise remained in the bar with the Beardens. 'Poor Cash is tight,' she said. And then, 'He told me this afternoon that he was going to paint the storm windows,' she said. 'Well, he mixed the paint and washed the brushes and put on some old fatigues and went into the cellar. There was a telephone call for him at around five, and when I went down to tell him, do you know what he was doing? He was just sitting there in the dark with a cocktail shaker. He hadn't touched the storm windows. He was just sitting there in the dark, drinking Martinis.'

'Poor Cash,' Trace said.

'You ought to get a job,' Lucy said. 'That would give you emotional and financial independence.' As she spoke, they all heard the noise of furniture being moved around in the lounge.

'Oh, my God!' Louise said. 'He's going to run the race. Stop him, Trace, stop him! He'll hurt himself. He'll kill himself!'

They all went to the door of the lounge. Louise again asked Trace to interfere, but she could see by Cash's face that he was way beyond remonstrating with. A few couples left the dance floor and stood watching the preparations. Trace didn't try to stop Cash – he helped him. There was no pistol, so he slammed a couple of books together for the start.

Over the sofa went Cash, over the coffee table, the lamp table, the fire screen, and the hassock. All his grace and strength seemed to have returned to him. He cleared the big sofa at the end of the room and instead of stopping there, he turned and started back over the course. His face was strained. His mouth hung open. The tendons of his neck protruded hideously. He made the hassock, the fire screen, the lamp table, and the coffee table. People held their breath when he approached the final sofa, but he cleared it and landed on his feet. There was some applause. Then he groaned and fell. Louise ran to his side. His clothes were soaked with sweat and he gasped for breath. She knelt down beside him and took his head in her lap and stroked his thin hair.

CASH HAD A terrible hangover on Sunday, and Louise let him sleep until it was nearly time for church. The family went off to Christ Church together at eleven, as they always did. Cash sang, prayed, and got to his knees, but the most he ever felt in church was that he stood outside the realm of God's infinite mercy, and, to tell the truth, he no more believed in the Father, the Son, and the Holy Ghost than does my bull terrier. They returned home at one to eat the overcooked meat and stony potatoes that were their customary Sunday lunch. At around five, the Parminters called up and asked them over for a drink. Louise didn't want to go, so Cash went alone. (Oh, those suburban Sunday nights, those Sunday-night blues! Those departing weekend guests, those stale cocktails, those half-dead flowers, those trips to Harmon to catch the Century, those postmortems and pickup suppers!) It was sultry and overcast. The dog days were beginning. He drank gin with the Parminters for an hour or two and then went over to the Townsends' for a drink. The Farquarsons called up the Townsends and asked them to come over and bring Cash with them, and at the Farquarsons' they had some more drinks and ate the leftover party food. The Farquarsons were glad to see that Cash seemed like himself again. It was half past ten or eleven when he got home. Louise was upstairs, cutting out of the current copy of *Life* those scenes of mayhem, disaster, and violent death that she felt might corrupt her children. She always did this. Cash came upstairs and spoke to her and then went down again. In a little while, she heard him moving the living-room furniture around. Then he called to her, and when she went down, he was standing at the foot of the stairs in his stocking feet, holding the pistol out to her. She had never fired it before, and the directions he gave her were not much help.

'Hurry up,' he said, 'I can't wait all night.'

He had forgotten to tell her about the safety, and when she pulled the trigger nothing happened.

'It's that little lever,' he said. 'Press that little lever.' Then, in his impatience, he hurdled the sofa anyhow.

The pistol went off and Louise got him in midair. She shot him dead.

JOHN CHEEVER WAS born in 1912. The son of a shoe salesman, Cheever enjoyed a somewhat idyllic childhood in the suburbs of Massachusetts before his father lost his fortune and fell to drinking. Frequently referred to as the Chekhov of these suburbs, Cheever published seven collections of stories and five novels throughout his lifetime, and was awarded the National Medal for Literature and the Pulitzer Prize, among others.

Cheever's own struggle with alcoholism is reflected in much of his writing. 'The Swimmer', which went on to become a major Hollywood movie featuring Burt Lancaster, portrays the grinding toll of suburban-ite socialising, while 'Goodbye, My Brother' and 'O Youth and Beauty!' depict the blind destruction that mindless drinking inflicts on families.

Cheever finally quit drinking in 1975. He died seven years later.

RECOMMENDED BOOKS BY JOHN CHEEVER:

Collected Stories
Falconer
The Wapshot Chronicle

How to detox after Drinking?

Swimming
ROGER DEAKIN

VINTAGE MINIS

Eating
NIGELLA LAWSON

VINTAGE MINIS

Calm
TIM PARKS

VINTAGE MINIS

Love
JEANETTE WINTERSON

VINTAGE MINIS

VINTAGE MINIS

The Vintage Minis bring you the world's greatest writers on the experiences that make us human. These stylish, entertaining little books explore the whole spectrum of life – from birth to death, and everything in between. Which means there's something here for everyone, whatever your story.

Desire	Haruki Murakami
Love	Jeanette Winterson
Babies	Anne Enright
Language	Xiaolu Guo
Motherhood	Helen Simpson
Fatherhood	Karl Ove Knausgaard
Summer	Laurie Lee
Jealousy	Marcel Proust
Sisters	Louisa May Alcott
Home	Salman Rushdie
Race	Toni Morrison
Liberty	Virginia Woolf
Swimming	Roger Deakin
Work	Joseph Heller
Depression	William Styron
Drinking	John Cheever
Eating	Nigella Lawson
Psychedelics	Aldous Huxley
Calm	Tim Parks
Death	Julian Barnes